Filling
the *Void*

Filling the *Void*

Nancy L. Bradbury

WESTBOW
PRESS

A DIVISION OF THOMAS NELSON

WestBow Press books may be ordered through booksellers or by contacting:

WestBow Press
A Division of Thomas Nelson
1663 Liberty Drive
Bloomington, IN 47403
www.westbowpress.com
1-(866) 928-1240

Because of the dynamic nature of the Internet, any web addresses or links contained in this book may have changed since publication and may no longer be valid. The views expressed in this work are solely those of the author and do not necessarily reflect the views of the publisher, and the publisher hereby disclaims any responsibility for them.

Certain stock imagery © Thinkstock.
Any people depicted in stock imagery provided by Thinkstock are models, and such images are being used for illustrative purposes only.

ISBN: 978-1-4497-5422-8 (sc)

Library of Congress Control Number: 2012909251

Printed in the United States of America

WestBow Press rev. date: 6/11/2012

I DEDICATE THIS BOOK to my loving husband and eternal friend Gene Bradbury. Gene was a college professor who gave his all to make a difference in the lives of his students. Professor Bradbury was more than a teacher; he was a motivator that encouraged with a firm and loving hand. He was adored by his students and all who had the privilege to know him. Gene was wise and prudent in every aspect of his life. I will be eternally thankful for the way he looked past all my imperfections.

He will always be remembered as a loving husband, father and grandfather and will be eternally missed. Gene left this world the same way he lived it: strong, humble and with a sound mind. His wisdom endured till the end and he left with a peace that gives me hope.

I first and foremost give thanks to my Lord and Savior Jesus Christ who by His Word leads me in my day to day existence. In addition, I give total credit to the Holy Spirit who gave me both inspiration and knowledge to become a writer. I would like to acknowledge my pastor Stacy Dingess whose sermons continue to inspire and enlighten me each week with new insight into God's Word. Finally, special thanks to my good friend Scott Arnold whom I admire and so graciously edited my manuscript.

CONTENTS

CHAPTER 1

Emotionally Empty

Everyone who has a breath has a longing for something to fill the emptiness that dwells in each of us. We feel this from the time of our first memory. As young children we want attention. So, because we have the inability to ask for attention; we get it anyway that works. At an early age we learn to lie and manipulate our parents into compliance. It comes as naturally as learning to walk and talk. We are searching for acceptance and assurance that we are important, that we matter. The teenage years brings a rebellious spirit against everything and everybody. Discipline is resisted, but very much desired. Why does this happen?

There are no set guidelines that parents can follow to insure that a child will grow up productive and emotionally healthy. All we can do is our best with what we have and hope for good results. Parents who devote all their time and energy to their children sometimes face devastating results. On the other hand, parents who neglect and ignore their children sometimes have children who excel. Much research has been done on innate verses environment, but nothing has given a concrete answer. So, we come back to the void which lurks inside us that yearns to be filled. We search for that missing link that completes us. What is it that we search for in the mist of this human existence?

What we are really looking for is Love. But, when we can not get the love our soul yearns for we turn to other things to fill the void. There are just a few who escape the experiences which I speak of in this book. Those who do escape the behaviors still feel the void sometime during their life. The void is described as a longing for something to satisfy our existence.

The void manifests in most of us through unhealthy relationships and selfish behaviors. We live for ourselves and embrace all the world sees as acceptable. Our morals and values are non-existent, or at least obscured by our worldly views. Lying becomes a habit to fill our selfish behavior and is not given a second thought. We say what we want, when we want. When someone asks us why, we just respond with "I don't know". I believe there is some truth to this statement, "I don't know". We really don't know why we act the way we act. But the answer should be because "I have a void and I need to fill it and until then my behavior is going to be out of my control".

We hurt those who care for us and never expect consequences. When there are consequences for our selfish, and sometimes illegal actions we just blame it on our past. We have the attitude that reflects our inability to take personal responsibility. Our actions are sometimes blamed on how we grew up or how we were treated by others. Any reason will do because most of the time we don't know. If we do know, we don't want to say, because we are selfish. Selfish is what we are, and our thinking is "What is in it for me?"

So when we get caught up in our web of selfishness we deny our responsibility. We have a personal "pity party" and resume our lives in a manner of I don't care.

The family has deteriorated to the point that our children have become fatherless and motherless. The average family of today is not only single parent homes; but, consists of homes where there are stepmothers, stepfathers and stepchildren who try to intermingle. There are many homes that have parents who are living with a partner, sometimes even in homosexual relationships. Children are exposed to parents changing partners several times during their childhood. Many homes have drug or alcohol use by someone in the house. Homes are filled with chaos and confusion with daily screaming and arguing. Children are exposed to so much dysfunction that they find it normal and reflect that in their behavior. Today's family lifestyle can cause children to experience a "crummy life" syndrome. Looking at this picture of today's American family tends to shed a light on why our children are refusing to take responsibility for their actions.

The court system even supports the blame it on what I call the "crummy life syndrome". The jails are overcrowded and the cost of housing inmates is sky rocking. Drug crimes are at an all time high and increasing daily. If drugs are involved, a short stay in a rehab and you are free to continue with your crummy life. In recent years the court system have developed drug courts where restrictions are placed upon the drug offender but he or she is kept on the street. There are many programs that attempt to help the disadvantaged, addicted criminal; but, none seem to be long term solutions. A system that began with one nation under God has taken on a new look in America. At least our money still bears the insignia of In God We Trust.

I am a high school teacher in the public school system. Everyday I have contact with teenagers who lack hope. Our school system is a good example of how we fail our youth who are involved in misconduct and sometimes refusal to follow rules. It takes too long in the court system to require restrictions on children who refuse to follow rules. So, we just give up and label them as kids with "Special Needs". Children usually drop out before they can acquire services to help them anyway. Many of the children are involved in drugs and inappropriate behaviors that continue into their adult life.

We label children that do not fit our perception of what we believe to be the "norm". The norm looks much different than it did in the past. Many children are given medication to calm them down and teachers are not even informed. Schools have given children the freedom of expression even to the extent that bisexual and homosexuality are considered normal and accepted. Not only are they accepted, but they are fostered by permission to openly dress and proclaim their differences. Schools do not mention the morals and values that this country was founded on. And of course we have separation of church and state, so the mention of God is prohibited and sometimes punished.

Character education made a short visit to our school system a decade ago, but it was thrown by the wayside just like Home Economics as part of the curriculum. The arts are the first programs to be cut when budgets get tight. Our children need more math and science to prepare them for the future. What a waste!! Our children go to school 1260 hours a year and receive little to prepare them for society. They are plunged into a culture that has adopted the attitude of "anything goes". That attitude is certainly reflected in appearance and behaviors.

Society even recognizes and enables the "crummy life" excuse. There are entire communities that are known for their crime rate and drug abuse. We live in communities where we do not even know our neighbors. This is amazing, knowing that just several decades ago that our neighbors were like family. Now most Americans don't even know who lives in the house next door. There are neighborhoods that are crippled by the choices made and have never known anything but poverty and despair. These communities are filled with people who have little or no hope of ever changing their circumstances.

The government is a big supporter of living the "crummy life". It issues checks every month to people who just "lay on the system". There are people who need aid and a hand-up. But, the government gives billions of taxpayer's dollars in the form of checks, medical insurance and housing because these "crummy-life syndrome" people are not able to or even unwilling to be productive members of society. In exchange they continue their destructive behaviors and refuse to cooperate with the most basic of rules. Well, you know the story - get a check and keep having children who suffer the poverty of your parents' destructive behaviors. Again there are programs; but, the system seems just to enable the behavior and sometime increase it.

The world is an enticing place and provides all kinds of temptations and pleasures. It offers an "escape" for the void that we feel. The escape is temporary and we have to keep filling it with whatever we can to keep us satisfied. Sometimes our desire to be satisfied can take us into a darkness in which we feel there is no escape. This is when we get caught up in oppression, addiction or depression. This type of escape is increasing rapidly in America where drug overdoses and suicides have become common and drug-related crimes seem to increase daily.

Oppression is defined as the feeling of being heavily burdened, mentally or physically, by troubles, adverse conditions, and anxiety. The trouble that haunts today's generation is caused by the inability to believe in something more that what they see. There are many in society today who have never experienced authentic love. Those who have are so caught up in pursuing and conforming to the world that they don't recognize or accept the love that is offered. It is no wonder that oppression has become commonplace because when love is absent, so is hope.

I see hopelessness on a daily basis as I talk with teenagers. There are several teenagers whom have shared with me their internal feelings about life. Kristin is a student who is an example of oppression. She feels a heavy burden to be accepted by her peers and often conveys that she is unloved and not worthy of praise or acceptance. She wants to be accepted but dresses and behaves in a manner that sets her apart. This is because she wants to be different in order to be noticed. Kristin's behavior is typical of today's teenagers who just want to feel important and fill the void that leaves them unsatisfied. Tori shared with me her feelings about why she wanted to get a tattoo. She says she wants something just for her, something personal. She, says that friends and even family are just temporary and will leave you; but a tattoo will always be with her. This clearly shows that she is looking for something to fill the void in her life. We all seek what Tori seeks - something permanent and personal.

These girls are just two examples of how people seek to fill the void. The most prevalent is drugs. It seems like everyone takes a pill to make them feel better and function in their day to day lives. The doctor offices are full of people looking for something artificial to help them "cope". Depression is extremely common. Drug abuse has hit an all time high and Americans are using anything and everything to get "high". Drug related deaths have become so common that most people know someone who has died because of drugs. Americans are inventing new drugs and even using commonly used household products to escape the emptiness they feel. Try watching the news and taking notes on its content. After a while you will begin to believe that there is no hope.

We create a world for ourselves that gives us temporary relief from the emptiness that plagues us all. Our minds tell us there is no hope. We are convinced that life is too hard or we blame it on our childhood or someone who disappointed or hurt us. Our ability to take responsibility for our actions is rare. Some people just refuse to think about it at all and have a genuine belief that life is just temporary, so live it up while you can. We see it in the clothing, piercings, tattoos and mutilation of their bodies. Attitudes about ourselves are deteriorating because we don't believe in anything except "now". This is just a deception created by the master of deceit.

Regardless of who we are and what environment we are exposed to, we all have the same longings and desires. There is a desire to belong and we mostly conform to whatever the environment around us says is acceptable. In our rebellious years we want to explore our individuality, and conformity is far from our minds. Either way, we are grouping in the darkness for whatever we can find to make us feel as if our lives mean something. We lack hope which descends us deeper into a hole where we see no solution.

Hope becomes nothing more than a wish list that we feel is unattainable. Hope is attainable and it surfaces from time to time to give us the ability to persevere through the difficult times. Lack of hope causes depression and makes us live our lives as helpless victims of deceit. When hope does come, we are plunged into a whole new dimension. Joy swells up inside us and things don't seem so impossible anymore. Hope changes our perspective and reveals the possibility that whatever we are seeking is possible. We all have stories where we felt helpless to change our circumstances. We lack hope that there is something more than the existence that we experience in day to day life in a world that embraces dysfunction.

There are many self help books and videos eager to give a solution to the hopelessness we feel; but, the end result is we still continue on the path of destruction. The only help comes from inside and the desire to find a greater purpose than just existence. There are so many people offering so many solution it is sometimes overwhelming. We feel isolated and are convinced that no one knows what we are experiencing. We turn to councilors, psychiatrists and psychologists who dwell into our past and reveal all our deep, dark secrets in hopes of finding relief. The professionals dig up memories in most cases that do us more harm than good. We go on medication to help with the symptoms and keep going through life lost and empty. Sometimes we even get addicted to the medications, which cause us additional problems to solve. There is no wonder we can't find the root problem.

Masking the emptiness or filling it with artificial substitute just gives temporary relief. Eventually we realize that there must be another way, so we jump to the next fad that promises to give us what we need. So, where does it stop and what do we do to once and for all fill the void lurking deep within all of us? Just hold on and know that the answer has always been there you just did not know where to look. Your eyes have been closed and ears have been deaf to the truth that fills the void. You have been deceived into thinking that this world is your home. To understand why America is experiencing such a hard time lets look at how in just the past four generations things have changed in America. America has birthed a generation who are experiencing a deeper void than ever before.

CHAPTER 2

An Entitled Generation

Let's take a look at another aspect of American life. Seldom today do we find a family consisting of a mother, father and children. It is even rarer to find a man and a woman who are married and raising the children who they conceived and birthed. Today's homes consist of mainly a mother raising children alone or homes where both the mother and father are employed full time. Children who grow up in such a home more commonly have neither parent invested in them. This makes materialistic possessions given by materialistic parents even more important to give these empty children something to hold onto. Giving possessions instead of time and love gives a person an obscured sense of happiness. Time with the family is the most important gift. Family relationships are a necessity for nurturing healthy behaviors in children.

In America we are raising a generation who seems to think that the world owes them something. Parents and grandparents seem to have bought into the idea that our children have to have "stuff".

Single parents sometimes work two jobs to give their children the best. What we are doing is trying to compensate for the absent parent or making sure our children have what the world says is necessary. Those children who don't have these materialistic possessions are ridiculed and teased. America is truly a materialistic society.

I know that the need to fit in has always been the way of life in America. But, the deterioration of the family has made this generation display behaviors that lead to life altering consequences. Teenagers and even preteens are under so much pressure that any morals or values taught are tossed out the window by peer influence. Children start this behavior at an early age and parents allow the behavior. This is mainly due to the fact that they do not have the energy to fight with children. There are children who have been a sweet and mild mannered child but become disrespectful, selfish and uncooperative teens.

What is a parent to do when they face this opposition? What parents should do is hold their ground and love the child through the situation. But, what is done too often is parents take an attitude of whatever works to get them to just shut up. There is no consistency because we are worn out and worn down trying to work and raise a family by ourselves or with two working parents trying to make ends meet. So, we have created an "entitled generation".

The "entitled generation" has a materialistic worldview. They must have the name brand clothing and whatever the fad is for this season. What ever the other kids have they must have it and they don't ask, they demand! So, parents work harder or go in debt to get the children what they demand so that their children will not get angry or become outcasts. Most of the time parents develop stress because they are overwhelmed by the demands of their children.

It is getting to be more and more expensive to give into the demands of our children. The items they want now are expensive brand name clothing and electronics such as video gaming systems, high priced phones, and other electronic gadgets. Parents feel an accomplishment when they can purchase these items for their children. It makes the parents happy to see that they are able to provide **stuff.** What parents do not realize is that these gadgets do not make chlidren happy; it is just a substitute for what children really want. The electronics parents work so hard to give their children just make children more withdrawn and non-communicative. These communication tools also allow them to participate in dangerous conversations and share inappropriate pictures and videos.

Most parents do not monitor their children's use of these electronics because they do not know how or they just do not have the time or energy. A disturbing reason is that it occupies their time and with the overwhelming lifestyles we have created we consider this a good thing. After all we are not arguing with them or having to confront yet another demand. The truth is *we have given them the very tools they need to participate in things we do our best to protect them from.*

Americans base good parenting on what they can provide for their children in the way of materialistic things. We still live in a capitalist economy. Although in recent days there has been a nationwide rebellion called "occupy wall street" movement. If you have not heard of this movement, let me explain. In cities across this country there have been protests by an ignorant generation who believe that capitalism is not fair. These naive individuals are protesting because they have a void. They don't really know or don't care about the principles on which this country was founded. They advocate that American wealth should be distributed among the people, namely the people who want a handout, not a hand up. Distribution of wealth is not capitalism!

This Entitled Generation, as they are called, feels they are entitled to be taken care of with free health care, and aid that would allow them to live on the system. That sounds like socialism or even communism. Most of the individuals who participate in these protests can not even answer economic questions about our nation's government. This is because they are ignorant to the governmental system in which they live. So, why are they there? They want to fill the void in their life. They are not acting in their own accord. They are being controlled and financed by organizations and others who seek to destroy capitalism.

This is the entitled generation who are searching for meaning to their life. They follow whoever will offer them what they want, which is something to fill the void. They are being deceived by those who know how to manipulate the weak. Most of the participates in this so-called protest are young impressionable people who have grown up in a world where everything was given to them and now they don't have a clue of what to do when the support runs out. Most are unemployed or underemployed and are unable to compete in a workplace that demands accountability and skills. Even though most of the individuals have an education, they lack work ethic and vision to survive in a capitalist economy.

A typical profile of the entitled generation is a skewed concept of moral character mixed with an upbringing that has left them helpless victims of society. Basic causes are their dysfunctional families, television and a society who has condoned their behavior. Television depicts homosexuality as a normal and acceptable way of life. Cursing and bad behavior are glorified, promoted as accepted. Cartoons have become rude, obnoxious and morally degradable. Parents set their children in front of a television and desensitize them to improper behaviors.

Most children spend their time watching secular television, surfing the Internet and communicating through text and facebook. But, they lack communication skills needed to function in society. Children are using this means of communication at a very early age. Children as young as seven have a facebook. Face to face communication is extremely difficult for them. They do not make eye contact and a two-way conversation is rare. Texting is a way of communicating even if they are in the same room or the same car. They have become introverts who can not hold a productive verbal conversation.

The school system attempts to control electronics; but, the truth is they don't do a very good job. The Internet is in most classrooms in America and although Facebook and messaging programs are blocked, students are the first to find a back door. The classroom atmosphere is so much different today. Teachers are overwhelmed with non-attentive children which cause them to tolerate more than they ever have before. Many students have individualized educational plans that must be adapted and many who do not have plans need them.

So, teachers have to adapt lessons to different levels of learners. Whether or not students are encouraged and given the individual attention needed to master the curriculum depends on class size.

Some children are placed in classrooms and cannot even read the material. Most classrooms are filled with disruptions, distractions and discipline problems. This brings us to the next attribute of the "entitled generation" and that is *lack of interest.*

It is not just school that has lost the interest of this generation; it is society in general. This generation is unlike the rebellion of former generations. The respect level is almost non-existent. I am not putting the blame on the generation itself because they grew up in a society with little or no rules that were consistent. Their role models were seen on a television screen or members of a dysfunctional family. Therefore, they have become selfish, thoughtless, angry and uncooperative people. Drugs have become so common that someone not taking drugs is labeled the exception. Drugs have always been around in past generations; but, not to the extent that they take lives, every day.

There is such a void in the lives of this generation that they will take a pill to fit into the norm. Some will say they take drugs to lessen the stress or give them an escape from their life. They do not have the imagination or creativity that enables them to occupy their mind. This is caused by the constant need by parents to entertain them with materialistic *stuff.* The things children do today does very little to enable them to use their minds or communicate in any way. Video games are mindless actions that only requires minimal hand and eye coordination. Television shows today depicts a worldview that glorifies that "anything goes" attitude. Telephones and electronic gadgets allow them to have little or no personal contact with each other. They have become socialites without personalities.

What concerns me most is their blatant disregard for others. This selfish behavior is overwhelming parents and grandparents to the extent that they either give up and give in or become the victims of abuse. Yes, I said abuse! Because there are many parents and grandparents who are suffering abuse from the children whom they have raised. The disrespect has hit a level where compromise has turned into the children running the households. So, what is the answer for this entitled generation? First, we need to look at the problem and what this generation really wants. It is not the latest electronic device, name brand clothes or any of the *stuff* the world says makes them acceptable. It is simply *time* and *love*.

We all have grown up in this world that says we must have things to make us accepted. But, we have not been exposed to the level of mind altering media that has been generated to this generation. The youth of today are exposed to the world in a way that causes them to believe that they know the answers. Any attempts to move these youth in the right direction, is just wrong. The mindset is that we want what we want and will do whatever it takes to make people understand that we are right. Every generation has had problems with rebellion and selfishness. Although I grew up poor and cannot relate to the entitled generation, I can relate to the behaviors they possess.

CHAPTER 3

Living in Darkness

My story was one of conformity and selfish behaviors that led me into darkness and shielded me from any light that may have tried to penetrate my armor. Like many others I chose the wrong path and pursued a life that the world had to offer. I was deceived most of my life into thinking the world was my playground. At the age of eighteen I left home thinking that freedom was all I needed to be happy. I decided that I would make the decisions.

I was ignorant and had little concern for the pain I inflicted on others. I wasn't making my own decision; most of the time I let others control me. The deception led me to think that this was the way my life was and I conformed very well; but, I always felt there was more. I can remember the times when I actually said to myself there must be more. I look back on my life and remember dark days when the loneliness almost overwhelmed me. I was so desperate for any remnant of love that I would chase anything that gave me emotional or physical relief and made me *feel*. The love

I speak of was the love that one finds from inside and does not come from others. I had a loving mother. She loved me and told me often; but, somehow I lacked authentic love.

Everything that I pursued was temporary and left me wandering in the darkness with the same emptiness. In my most desperate times when I felt hopelessness, a comfort engulfed me that I did not recognize or could not explain. It felt like the arms of my mother were around me gently stoking my head. There were times that I know it would have been the end of me; but, somehow I persevered and survived. I always had that little voice that told me right from wrong; but, I ignored it because the world's pleasures ruled my life. I enjoyed the deceit and rejoiced in my wrongdoings most of the time. Seldom did I feel guilt or think that what I was doing was anything but normal.

Normal is a word that I do not understand. What is normal? Who defines normal? It is defined as conforming to the standard or the common type; usual not abnormal. I see many abnormal behaviors that are accepted and considered the standard. So, we conform to our common type and the people and environment around us. This use of the word normal justifies the saying, "you are judged by the company you keep". Our environment has much to do with how we view this word normal. Our lives are full of distractions which cause us to be blinded to what is really important. I never was one to waste time thinking about the future. The present kept me busy and I lived each day with the attitude that life was good.

Most of my adult life was spent searching for a way to satisfy my desires. In the beginning it was to satisfy the body. Then, it was to satisfy the emptiness. Finally, it was to satisfy the soul. My desires changed over the years, but even education, money and acceptance could not fill the void in my soul. I was focused on what the world had to offer and I rarely strayed from my human desires.

I filled the void with whatever at the time kept me happy. I always thought that the next relationship or another degree or more money would take away the emptiness; but, nothing worked for very long. I was blinded by lack of knowledge and reluctance to hear anything that was not to my benefit. My selfishness was my only friend and the world was my home. My story is typical of one searching for love in all the wrong places.

The attraction to superhero and supernatural movies is phenomenal. Watch the reviews of movies that display a superhero of supernatural theme and watch the people flock to watch. We humans love the extraordinary. Most people will say that they believe in ghosts or spirits. Some people believe in UFO's and aliens. We humans innately know there is something more than our existence here on the earth. My beliefs varied throughout my life according to my environment.

I was always fascinated with the supernatural. I remember as a young girl having a book on white witchcraft. Television shows and movies about the supernatural world always fascinated me. That is as far as it went. I always stopped short of involving myself in rituals or spells; although, I did go to a palm reader a couple of times. I played with and Ouija board once and became frightened and threw it away. But, I did pursue the lusts and pleasures of the world that lead to destructive behaviors.

In my twenties I participated in a seven year marriage to a man who physically and emotional abused me. These years were filled with worldly pleasures and heartbreaking pain. If opportunity did knock I did not recognize it because of my bondage. My desire for attention and love caused me to compromise myself on many occasions. My destructive behaviors destroyed any self worth and yielded me helpless to dig myself out of the hole I had created. Had I gone too far? How would I know because I was blind to the truth or any resemblance of what was acceptable? I had made my bed and now I lay in it as a willing participant.

The years passed and I became complacent to the fact that this is what life was and acceptance was the only answer. I continued to make one bad decision after another. Until, I woke up broke, hungry and without running water. My desperate situation brought me once again to the thought that there must be something more. I was engaged in a battle of directions or what I call the Valley of Decision. In one direction was the difficult and almost unthinkable and unattainable choice. In the other direction there was the uncomfortable life I had come accustomed too.

I grew up in a family of seven, me being the youngest. We lived on welfare and my dad was a drunk and wife abuser. My mother was loving and kind and did what she knew how to give us love with discipline. I was the only one who graduated from high school. Probably because my father died when I was thirteen and left my mother to raise the three children she still had at home. My mother died when I was nineteen, which left me an orphan.

I don't remember much about my childhood which I consider a good thing. I have never considered searching for missing childhood memories. My sister also has gaps in her childhood memories. I would have to say that what childhood memories I have are what I considered at the time *normal*. We were poor; but, so was most everybody else we knew. I never had any expectations of going to college or pulling myself out of poverty. In fact, a life on the system was what I knew and work did not fit into my view of the world. I worked a short time at a job after high school; but, it got in my way of my distorted perception for personal independence.

I have always heard the window of opportunity opens within your lifetime and it is up to you to climb through it. Looking back I did see windows; but I only thought they were for someone else. Looking through them was all that I could bring myself to do. I had spent my twenties in chains, bound by my insecurities and inability to see past my limitations. My limitations began to change when I took a computer class at the local vocational school. Next, I enrolled in a couple of accounting classes trying to learn to keep the books for my husband's construction business. What a surprise when I was able to excel and even help others in class. This gave me the self esteem to believe that just maybe I was college material. I applied for a college grant and my life began to turn around.

The day did finally come when I recognized an opportunity to change my life. I was thirty-two years old and living a selfish, nonproductive life. I had always wanted to pursue an education, but I was imprisoned and bound by the world. I was bound by my own selfish lusts and was not willing to budge even though the prison door was open. It wasn't easy to climb out of the hole I had dug. Temptation hit me at every corner; but, I just kept walking because I finally saw the hope for an almost perfect life.

CHAPTER 4

Turning on the Light

It was a warm August morning when I received the letter that gave me the resources to start college. I quickly took the chance and enrolled full time at the local community college. This was the pivotal moment when my decision making began to change my life for the better. The decisions I made from that day lead me to a place that opened the door for opportunity. I was able to continue my education because of the man that would later become my husband. He was a professor and twenty-four years my senior. We fell in love within the first six months. He taught me proper grammar and proper behavior. I was so receptive to his teachings; I lacked guidance and welcomed someone who could give me more.

When the professor, Gene, and I were married, I thought this would fill the void. He was a wonderful man and husband. He spoiled me and gave me love like I had never known before. The level of respect and feeling of belonging was what made our marriage so grand. But, as I look back there was still something missing. We had a wonderful marriage, a nice home, nice cars, and added to our family my granddaughter who we adored. She gave us so much joy and life was almost perfect. My life kept me busy and the world was at my beckon call; but, I still had a longing in my heart.

My ability to see was so darkened that I believed I was living the American dream. My heart had become hardened by the betrayals of those around me and I had placed a wall between me and most everyone. Lack of trust and lack of forgiveness can destroy a soul. My husband and I were living a life the world would call abundant. All was well in our home and money flowed like water into our material possessions. My life was in my opinion almost perfect. Could life get any better? When we base our happiness upon what we have, we are sooner or later disappointed. Everything is temporary and almost perfect lives can be changed in a day.

My almost perfect life started to fall apart on a sunny May afternoon with an urgent call from my husband, Gene. He said, "you need to come home I am bleeding" "OK, I will be right there". I drove the two miles home with my flashers on wondering what I would find. I went in and found my husband on the couch looking fine. He said, "I have been throwing up blood." Thus began my awakening. I realized that my almost perfect life was falling apart and there was nothing I could do. Not my marriage or my love for my husband; but, the life that I thought was perfect was just a substitute and a preparation for the real journey.

My world come tumbling down two weeks later when my husband was diagnosed with lung cancer. That summer was full of both desperation and inspiration. I was losing my husband;

but, gaining a strength and love that I had never known. There is something about being desperate and helpless that makes you reevaluate your life. I would have to say even though this was the worst time in my life it was the best time in my life. I was going through the wilderness and had such a strength and peace that I had never known.

I remember just lying in bed crying out "please don't let him suffer". Who was I talking to? I had been living my life for me and I was doing just fine. My hard heart that had consumed my life was about to be humbled. Gene and I had become self sufficient and self reliant on ourselves. In our quest for happiness I had isolated myself and lived the almost perfect life.

The summer was long and solemn. The only lifeline was a coworker and soon to be my friend, Cassie was an ear for my desperate cries. She was always there to give me spiritual assurance that I would persevere. I remember sitting at the computer crying and mourning, communicating with the only one who seemed to give me any hope. She did not know it; she was only responding in the only way she knew. She never saw what was on the other side of the conversation. The words were all she saw; but, her responses were penetrating my soul and preparing me for the journey.

My husband of fifteen years went home to be with the Lord only five months after his initial phone call. He never suffered or had shortness of breath and died peacefully at home. My husband was a proud man and refused to let anyone see him in his deteriorating condition. He grew up in the church and knew God. He never shared much with me. He did tell me that when he was growing up, he had been in the in the church choir and was baptized. Three days before he went home he said, "God is going to be good to you". This gives me such peace now and assures me that he went home to be with the Lord. The memorial service was just as he requested and I said goodbye to my best friend and loving husband.

The following year was full of struggles and victories. I had never lived alone and now I had to make decisions and raise our twelve year old granddaughter. I had never been a reader prior to my husband's illness; I developed a hunger for reading over the summer. I began my reading with supernatural books about ghosts and mediums. By the time the summer was over, I had graduated my reading to spiritual books. I read anything I could on spirituality, still trying to fill a void. A friend gave me the book "90 Minutes in Heaven" and this started my quest for the truth.

I remembered that I always believed in God and knew about heaven and hell. I must have learned it somewhere in my forgotten childhood. The months passed and I went through the motions of living and working. Putting up the front that everything was good, I continued to teach, eat lunch, and converse with my coworkers. On the outside I was brave and productive; but on the inside I was so empty. Time had passed and my emptiness turned to hunger for something to fill the void in my life. So started the quest that changed my life and continues to satisfy the lifelong void.

Cassie, a friend and coworker, invited me to church where a long time friend was preaching on Wednesday nights. I accepted the invitation and it was the first time I began be exposed to the Word of God. I had gone to church a few times throughout my life; but did not even consider the Word of God more than a book I could not understand. Was this what I had longed for all my life? I was just going because I enjoyed Bill and he could also sing. I had never planned to get caught up in attending church. My greatest reluctance to going to church was the time it involved. Sunday was the day I got caught up on my household chores. I also felt that changing my life was impossible although I was a good person. I did not drink, curse or do the other things which, in my opinion, makes one bad. My life was going along just fine.

I had been going to Wednesday night services for about four weeks when Bill told us to open the Bible and pick one scripture and meditate on it until the next Wednesday. Wouldn't you know it, I open the Bible up to Psalms 23, you know "The Lord is my Shepherd…." I returned the next week and Bill said the words that would change my life forever. He made this statement: "I had a sermon prepared for tonight; but, the Holy Spirit placed upon my heart scriptures that I have preached on so many times. I have no choice but to be obedient. Open your Bibles to "Psalms 23". Who was this Holy Spirit? How did He know what I had been reading? I was shocked, excited and humbled. I never heard the sermon. My mind kept saying "How is this possible?" By the end of the service I knew that this was what I had longed for all my life. God spoke to me that night and said, "Come and I will show you that I am the Lord your God". I gave my heart and soul to the Lord that night. I surrendered my almost perfect life and become a new creature drafted into the kingdom of God.

My almost perfect life became extraordinary and full of miracles, signs and wonders. God led me to a church that far exceeded my expectation. I had never been exposed to church life so I had no preconceptions. The few churches I had attended were at best ordinary. I always sought the extraordinary and found it the first time I walked into the Penacostal church. The spirit of God was so strong it was hard to stand. I experienced for the first time in my life what God had tried to convey to me all my life. For the first time I felt a satisfaction, a completeness in my soul. This was definitely what I wanted to continue to experience.

I began to read the Bible and Christian books with a passion. I was driven by a force that was so strong I could hardly function in my day to day responsibilities. My time was consumed with learning and pursuing the truth. Television became a thing of the past except to watch Christian television. Conversations begin to change and my focus was on talking about the Bible or anything to do with my new found love. My time was spent going to church, conferences and prayer meetings. I would go anywhere I was invited to hear or experience more of what I had found. It was a wonderful, glorious and sometimes a challenging experience.

I had found a home church and put all my energy into learning more. I joined the ladies ministry, attended leadership training and put myself in any place where there was an opportunity to learn more. My faith and excitement was to the point that sometimes I could not contain it and it spilled over everywhere in my life. I was baptized on Valentines Day. How appropriate a day that exemplifies love and I got to proclaim to everyone my one and only love, Jesus. The first few months of my newfound life were glorious and driven; but this time period became the breath of life that changed me forever.

CHAPTER 5

Breath of Life

For the next year, I read every possible moment. My life was filled with blessing after blessing. Relationships were healed, desires were fulfilled and victories were won. Extraordinary things began to happen - like when I had major water leaks and they just disappeared with no explanation. Money started appearing in my bank account that I could not explain. Eventually, I just stopped trying to explain it and just realized it was God.

On one occasion, I was at the closing for my daughter's home and the lawyer said the sellers changed their mind and backed out. I was upset for about two minutes and I told the lawyer that I needed to pray and that they would go through with the sale. In about thirty minutes after leaving the bank, the realtor called and asked if I could come back to the bank to close. I am overwhelmed by the power and generosity of the God I serve.

My desire for the Word was insatiable. My desire for more led me to Kansas City. One of my Christian sisters told me that there was a revival going on at a church that was broadcast on television.

I went online and watched a service and we drove to Kansas City. It was great! About 300 people were in a sanctuary looking for the same experience. All the people had one thing on their mind, they wanted more. They wanted to step out of the ordinary and seek all God had to offer.

The trip to Kansas City was an experience I will always remember. Just being in a room with a group of people who were desperate for a manifestation of His presence was well worth the trip. My experience made me realize several things about my walk as a Christian. First, I realized that God will freely give to those who seek Him. Second, God is not a feeling; He is a presence that goes beyond a feeling. Lastly, God is omnipresent. He resides with you at all time whether you are alone or in a large group of believers. It is what you bring with you into the group of believers that determines what you take when you leave.

I have attended many services since I accepted the gift of salvation. Most have been extraordinary not because of the music or even the message; but because I went with expectations. Many people leave church the way they come. Many times it is pride that gets in the way of receiving what God wants for our lives. I have found myself resisting to surrender to a move of God. We worry to much about what people will think of us than following our true convictions.

I can never get used to the awesomeness of His mercy and grace. Matthew 7:7-11 gives us a look at His promise to His children. "Ask, and it shall be given you; seek, and ye shall find; knock, and it shall be opened unto you: For every one that asketh receiveth; and he that seeketh findeth; and to him that knocketh it shall be opened. Or what man is there of you, whom if his son ask bread, will he give him a stone? Or if he ask a fish, will he give him a serpent? If ye then, being evil, know how to give good gifts unto your children, how much more shall your Father which is in heaven give good things to them that ask him?"

I have experienced so many wonderful blessings from God that I could write a book just on blessings alone. But, the one that supersedes any other up to this point happened just a few months after I received salvation. It was a Sunday night and I was in Chapter two of a book on the Baptism of the Holy Ghost. It was the end of the service when the pastor said that to receive the Holy Ghost you must be in complete surrender. Then, he welcomed anyone who wished to receive the baptism of the Holy Ghost to come to the front. I ran to the front seeking all that my God had to offer. I was overcome with a sense of wonder and succumbed to His Will and power that night.

The next few days, following this experience, was so marvelous, satisfying and rewarding. I was assured that I had been endowed with the infilling of the Holy Ghost. I did not feel different or was I completely convinced of the authenticity of my experience. My greatest desire was to please the God who was so graciously bestowing upon me all that my heart could withstand. But, nothing could prepare or compare to what happened next.

The events of the next night after receiving the baptism of the Holy Ghost will always be crystal clear in my mind. Every detail of that experience will forever be a testimony to His loving kindness and tender mercies. I had just gone to bed and prayed as I always did before climbing into bed. I was lying in bed and had an experience that gave me conformation that what I had received was real. I found myself not breathing; but, fully conscience. Then, a voice in my mind, which was very clear, spoke to me and said, "Does this frighten you"? I replied, "No". Next, I took a breath that was so deep it seemed to fill my very soul. I could not move or open my eyes and felt a peace that surpassed all understanding. My experience ended by the Holy Spirit taking over and speaking in an unknown tongue. Still I was surrounded by the most peaceful, loving feeling that assured me that this was the Lord my God.

The following few days consisted of an overwhelming grief. I can only explain it by saying that it was as if I had lost someone dear to me. I would cry uncontrollably and feel as if I were in mourning. Looking back I realize that this was the process of purging my soul. I did lose someone, me; but what I got in return was far better and amazing. This experience gave me a new perspective on my life.

In the months that followed I would be awakened at 3 am as if for a reason. Night after night my sleep was interrupted and not understanding I would go back to sleep. I was attending a service of a well known evangelist and was looking through the merchandise on sale. I was looking at a CD called the third watch and ask the lady what it was about. She replied, "It is when the Heavens open at 3 am. She asked, have you ever been awakened at 3 am?" This was just one of the amazing ways God has in resolving unanswered questions. When we seek we will find. He always seems to answer questions through a song or a Christian program. Every sermon seemed to be speaking directly to me and music took on a new dimension. Music was only something I listened to in the car sometimes. Praise and worship music began to touch my spirit and I began to listen to it everyday.

I have had so many experiences in my Christian walk. I continue to be amazed by the way my Lord works. He always is generous and faithful to do what He promises. It doesn't always turn out the way I think it should; but, it always turns out better than I had imagined. I am blessed beyond measure and live the abundant life. I have times when the world throws me a curve and for a moment I pause or stumble; but He knows my voice. Sometimes all I can manage to do is cry for help or call His name. It does not take long until the peace that surpasses understanding envelops me and once again and I regain my joy. Oh, my greatest desire is to see eyes opened and hearts receptive to His marvelous love.

I compare my walk with the Lord like living in a world where most people are blind. You talk to them and try to explain what you see; but they cannot see or understand. I am convinced that the only way to get people to listen is through living your life as a living testimony to Jesus. They don't want to hear about Jesus. They want to hear how your life has changed since you found Jesus. Your testimony is powerful!

CHAPTER 6

He Said, "Come"

The Bible reads, Come unto me, all you that labour and are heavy laden, and I will give you rest (Matthew 11: 28). As sinners we believe that we need to fix something in our lives before we can come to our God. We tell ourselves that it would be too hard to be a Christian. We fool ourselves into believing that we are good people and God would not punish a good person. If we believe in God and do our best according the world then we will not be punished. After all, God is a forgiving God. Our perception is obscured by our worldview of Christianity. I say unto you, that likewise joy shall be in heaven over one sinner that repenteth, more than over ninety and nine just persons, which need no repentance (Luke 15:7).

The truth is we have a free will which God does not overpower. God has the power to convict our hearts; but in the end it is our decision to accept or reject the Gift of salvation. Well meaning Christians will tell you what you can and cannot do as a Christian. The commission of a Christian is to preach the gospel and tell people about Jesus and how He died on the cross for our sins. Christians should also share their testimonies at every opportunity. It is not, however, the Christian who tells what people should do or how anyone should act. God will convict them and guide them through their conversion.

Looking at the "normal" Christian today a sinner would be justified in their reluctant attitude to become one of them. 'For whosoever shall call upon the name of the Lord shall be saved" (Romans 10:13). Everyone is a whosoever. It does not matter what your circumstances are or what you have done the Lord says come. If you confess with your mouth that Jesus is Lord and believe in your heart that God raised him from the dead, you will be saved (Romans 10:9). The first words I actually heard from God was "Come and I will show you that I am the Lord your God". He just wants us to humbly come to Him and lay our burdens down.

There was a woman who received salvation in our church. She had attended church numerous times and at the end of the service she left in tears. The conviction to turn her life over to God was very real. Week after week she refused to surrender and ask God into her life. One morning she came to church and was obviously upset. Church had not begun yet and she set down on the front pew and stated that she did not know what to do. She took the Lord into her heart that morning and began a journey that she uses as her testimony. She had been addicted to drugs for ten years and was delivered that morning. Her desire to use drugs was instantly and divinely eliminated. Her mind wanted the drug but she never went through physical withdraws. The mind is a powerful part of the flesh. It convinces you that you need something when you know you don't.

Two weeks later God delivered her from cigarette addiction. She was changed and you could see it not only in her actions but in her physical appearance. A troubled and confused appearance turned to a smile and joy. There is an excitement in her that is contagious. Her testimony is just one of many of those who surrender to conviction and allow God to change their lives.

When God pours out His Grace and Mercy and gives us salvation, there should be an immediate change. Our attitude and desires should be different. Sin becomes more difficult. This is because the Holy Spirit is without sin and now He dwells in us. The flesh still has the desire; but the Holy Spirit is convicting of any wrong behaviors. The devil steps in and starts putting thoughts in your head that are not real. Sometimes confusion sets in and pressures from friends and even family crushes your excitement. There are some who do not understand the conflict they experience. You desire to go on with your life; but somehow it feels different when you sin. Sin is something you no longer desire to participate in and you are overwhelmed with conviction. If you ignore the conviction and continue to participate in sinful behaviors the Holy Spirit will withdraw and allow you to exert your free will. Your walk with God will just be short and you will be allowed to go back to your worldly, sinful existence.

"This I say then, Walk in the Spirit, and ye shall not fulfill the lust of the flesh" (Galatians 5:16). There are seventeen works of the flesh listed in Galatians 5:19-21 (adultery, fornication, uncleanness, lasciviousness, idolatry, witchcraft, hatred, variance, emulations, wrath, strife, seditions, heresies, envying, murders, drunkenness, reveling and such things). It is written that "they which do such things shall not inherit the kingdom of God" (Galatians 5:21).

Gods Word is not negotiable and those who practice these lusts retain sin in their lives and will not enter Heaven. You will not inherit the kingdom of God even if you are calling yourself a Christian. The flesh is very powerful and if you continue to give in, then the Holy Spirit will let you have it your way. On the other hand, if you began to turn away from sin then the Holy Spirit wins.

When we walk in the Spirit we possess the fruits of the Spirit. There are nine fruits of the Spirit listed in Galatians 5: 22-23. "But the fruit of the Spirit is love, joy, peace, longsuffering, gentleness, goodness, faith, meekness, temperance…." Christians are identified by these fruits. Christians who do not display these fruits should seek a more intimate relationship with God. The fruits should be evident and consistent. And ye shall seek me, and find [me], when ye shall search for me with all your heart (Jeremiah 29:13). When we seek Him with all our heart we will find the fruits and they will be a part of our everyday life. We should never have to try to display these fruits; they come just as natural as getting out of bed in the morning.

There are many who are saved only to turn back to sin almost immediately. The flesh overpowers them and they give in too quickly to their fleshly, worldly behaviors. "Put to death therefore what is earthly in you: sexual immorality, impurity, passion, evil desire, and covetousness, which is idolatry. On account of these the wrath of God is coming" (Colossians 3:5-6). The unwillingness to give up our sin will cause us to fall back into the hands of our adversary. We will never be prefect. Christians make mistakes and sin. The problem arises when we are unwilling to change and give up worldly desires. We are children of light.

"Then Jesus said unto them, Yet a little while is the light with you. Walk while you have the light, lest darkness come upon you: for he that walketh in darkness knoweth not whither he goeth. While you have light, believe in the light, that you may be the children of light" (John 12:35-36)

Salvation came with a price and turning to God is a serious decision. "For ye are "bought" with a price: therefore glorify God in your body, and in your spirit, which are God's" (1 Corinthians 6:20). Jesus paid the price on the cross for our sins. Salvation is free and can only be obtained through admission of our sins and belief that He died, was resurrected and awaits us at the right hand of the Father.

Changes will happen in your life and you will find it difficult to live your life as you did before you accepted Jesus Christ. It is great when you receive salvation. The angels in heaven rejoice when a sinner accepts Jesus. "say unto you, that likewise joy shall be in heaven over one sinner that repenteth, more than over ninety and nine just persons, which need no repentance" (Luke 15:7). As a Christian we need to realize that we have a responsibility to turn away from sin. There must be a visible sign of change when salvation is accepted. If you and others can not see a change in your attitude and actions then the chances are you did not accept the gift of salvation.

There is an instant change that cannot be denied. Other changes take a little longer and can come gradually. Either way the difference in your attitude is apparent to all who knew you before salvation. Some people are delivered from drug addiction or smoking the moment they receive salvation. Some are healed of disease or pain. And still others have to work at giving up such addictions or habits. Either way, the Holy Spirit convicts the new found Christian of sin that has controlled their lives. The new found Christian does not have to be told what a sin is because the Holy Spirit will make them aware of what is right and what is wrong.

CHAPTER 7

Surrender to Change

The day I received Jesus into my heart I began to change. It seemed as if the world had been rearranged and what I thought I liked started to become uninteresting. Television is a good example of what I enjoyed but it became uncomfortable to watch. As a sinner, I liked talk shows and programs on the supernatural. But, when I watched my favorite shows it felt different. Instead, I wanted to read books on spirituality and go to church services. I wanted to do anything that placed me in a position to learn more about my new found Love, Jesus. Jesus occupied my life and I wanted to be around people who would talk about Jesus. I was consumed by His presence and walked, talked and lived to serve Him. The world still existed and it went on just as it had always been; but I was focused on Him.

Living a Christian life takes sacrifice and surrendering your control to the Savior. Surrendering control is the most difficult of all because most of us are raised to be independent. From a young age we are taught that we should be in control of our own lives.

Men especially are told to keep control and women are taught not to be submissive to anyone. Becoming a Christian throws all that out the window and have to come to the conclusion that they are not in control. We are asked to give up our independence and completely rely on God for everything. Surrendering all is where most Christians draw the line. They surrender some and try to control there lives themselves. "If any man will come after me, let him deny himself and take up his cross and follow me" (Matthew 16:24).

Many people will say that they believe that they will go to heaven when they die because they believe in God or they are a good person. These are sinners who lack knowledge that the only way is to accept the gift of salvation and turn from sin. They use an excuse like I am not ready or I am still young. They do not have ears to hear and their understanding is obscured by the master of deceit. Even more disturbing is that there are many Christians who do not proclaim their Christianity. You could be working with them and not know they are Christians.

Many people go to church and fill the seats on Sunday but desire what the world has to offer. "Love not the world, neither the things that are in the world. "If any man love the world, the love of the Father is not in him. For all that is in the world, the lust of the flesh. And the lust of the eyes, and the pride of life, is not of the Father, but is of the world" (1 John 2:15-16). Genesis 3:6 explains it best: And when the woman saw that the tree *was* good for food – the lust of the flesh and that it *was* pleasant to the eyes – the lust of the eyes and a tree to be desired to make *one* wise – the pride of life. She took of the fruit thereof, and did eat, and gave also unto her husband with her; and he did eat." We can be deceived when we depend on our fleshly senses (smell, touch, hearing, sight, taste).

We must live and exist in this world as Christians; but we must set ourselves apart and walk in the Spirit. We live in a world that demands our time and energy. Don't give the world too much time and energy or it will consume and confuse you into thinking it has something to offer you. "Be sober, be vigilant; because your adversary the devil, as a roaring lion, walketh about, seeking whom he may devour" (1 Peter 5:8). The devil is constantly searching for people who are weak in their faith. He deceives them into compromising their morals and values. He has studied us since the day we were conceived. He knows how to tempt us and what makes us tick. When you become a new creature in Christ the devil is confused. The person he knew no longer exists and it is extremely hard for him to attack and control you in the ways he has become accustomed to. Your reactions and desires are different. Everything he knew just got thrown out with all the sin. Do not deceive yourself because he continues to look at your weakness and never gives up. Just know that your strength comes from the Lord and how you pursue your new found life.

Do not be conformed to this world, but be transformed by the renewal of your mind, that you may prove what is good and acceptable and perfect will of God (Romans 12:2). We are supposed to be set apart as Christians. Wherefore come out from among them, and be ye separate, saith the Lord, and touch not the unclean thing; and I will receive you (2 Corinthians 17). So why is so hard to identify Christians outside the church doors? I believe it is fear of being set apart or not fitting in. "He said to them, "You are the ones who justify yourselves in the eyes of men, but God knows your hearts. What is highly valued among men is detestable in God's sight." (Luke 16:15)

A Christian has the reputation of Jesus to uphold. How we conduct ourselves is a reflection on our Savior. If you choose behaviors that are not pleasing to God then you not only sin but you must step over the cross. Our view of the world should be changed and our minds transformed to a different way of thinking. "And put on the new man, which is renewed in knowledge after the image of Him that created him". (Colossians 3:10)

Speak to a new Christian and they probably can not quote scripture; but they are so excited about their new found life. Their minds are being transformed and they welcome every moment and rejoice in every new experience. No one can discourage them or hold them back. They are upon the mountain and refuse to move. Nurtured, this enthusiasm will grow and explode over into the church and beyond. They want everyone to know what they have found and wonder why everyone is not excited and proclaiming His name. If only we could bottle this new found Christianity and release it upon request.

What happens in between that devotion and enthusiasm? God is the same, yesterday, today and forever. It is the Christian who drifts away from His presence. We cease to seek Him in a manner we first found Him. There are going to be tribulations. "These things I have spoken unto you, that in me you might have peace. In the world you shall have tribulation: but be of good cheer; I have overcome the world." (John 16:33) Oh if we would only seek Him daily, we would find that our Love for Him would grow and overflow. But we begin to give Him less and less time. You can spot those Christians who spend most of their time with Jesus.

These people are different, set apart. They seem to smile when there is nothing to smile about. They don't hang out and linger in conversations unless the conversation is about the kingdom of God. Most of the time conversations change when they arrive. These are the Christians who are called Fanatics. Jesus consumes their lives from the purses they carry to the stickers on their car. They seem to be on a mountain proclaiming the name of the Lord.

There is a way to keep this awestruck wonder. I have a friend who has been a Christian most of his life and every time I see him he has a smile and a story about the greatness of Jesus. He is always quoting scriptures and letting everyone know where he stands with his faith. I so enjoy talking with him, his enthusiasm for the Lord is contagious. Tempered with this enthusiasm is a humble demeanor. So what is his secret? The answer is simple, a close walk with God everyday!

The Bible states, … that in the last days perilous times shall come. For men shall be lovers of their own selves… "Having a form of godliness but denying the power thereof; from such turn away". Ever learning and never able to come to the knowledge of the truth (2 Timothy 3:1-7). This scripture is a perfect description of many Christians. They have a form of godliness. They go to church and play music and even proclaim they are Christians. Some are even active in the church as teachers or choir members. What does it mean to deny the power thereof? To deny the power means that outwardly they play the role of a Christian; but, the grace of God is not in their heart. They profess the scriptures to be the Word of God, yet they do not live the Word.

Every day Christians must make a conscious effort to be a light to the world. "Let your light so shine before men. That they may see your good works and glorify your Father which is in Heaven" (Matthew 5:16). The lost watch those who claim to be Christians and make judgments based on their behavior. Sinners often have reluctance about going to church because of the behaviors of people who call themselves Christians or attend church.

It is time for the Christian to stand up and accept the power that we have been given through the Lord Jesus Christ. "You shall know them by their fruits. Do men gather grapes of thorns, or figs of thistles (Matthew 7:16)?" This scripture is talking about Christians. We are told we are not suppose to judge; yet God said in 1 Corinthians 6:2 "Do ye not know that the saints shall judge the world? and if the world shall be judged by you, are ye unworthy to judge the smallest matters?"

Christians need to be aware of the fruits that fellow saints produce. The scriptures are clear when it comes to unbelievers. Be ye not unequally yoked together with unbelievers: for what fellowship hath righteousness with unrighteousness? and what communion hath light with darkness? (1 Corinthians 6:14). It is also written in 1Corinthians 5:11-13, "But now I have written unto you not to keep company, if any man that is called a brother be a fornicator, or covetous, or an idolator, or a railer, or a drunkard, or an extortioner; with such an one no not to eat". For what have I to do to judge them also that are without? do not ye judge them that are within? But them that are without God judgeth. Therefore put away from among yourselves that wicked person".

It is clear that we should not judge others; but, God has given us a sound mind and discernment to know the things we should do as saints. We need to be helpful forgiving and loving to those we call our brothers and sisters; however, we also need to be true to our conviction and follow the Word of God. The Word says put away from among the church those who call themselves Christian and are wicked.

CHAPTER 8

Worldly Christians

What happens to cause us to be complaisant Christians? We get comfortable and start conforming to what is "normal" behavior. Our love for God does not change. We still go to church and proclaim our love for our Savior. The Bible reads, "Enter by the narrow gate. For the gate is wide and the way is easy that leads to destruction, and those who enter by it are many. For the gate is narrow and the way is hard that leads to life, and those who find it are few" (Matthew 7:13-14). THOSE WHO FIND IT ARE FEW! The Bible has many scriptures that give us specific instructions on how to live our lives as Christians. We will never be perfect. We have Grace and Mercy that will follow us all the days of our lives. Our goal should be everyday to become holy. "You shall be holy, for I am holy." (1 Peter 1:16)

The normal Christian in America does not pray on a regular basis and devotes little time in the Word of God "The Holy Bible". Some Christians do not even attend church on a regular basis. The Holy Bible is specific on these areas of a Christian life. Pray without ceasing (1 Thessalonians 5:17). But he answered, "It is written, Man shall not live by bread alone, but by every Word that comes from the mouth of God" (Matthew 4:4). "Not forsaking the assembly of ourselves together, as the manner of some is; but exhorting one another, and so much the more as you see the day approaching" (Hebrews 10:25). Well the day is approaching! Ask any Christian "Do you believe that the end of the age is near?" They will respond with a resounding *yes* and even some sinners will respond with a yes.

Why do Christians find themselves following the normal model? It is because the world is a temptation. There is so much that demands our time. We spend most of our time doing what is most important to us. Think about how you spend most of your day and you will find what is most important. If you spend more than eight hours a day working, then work is important. Work becomes a problem when it stops being a way of support and starts being a way of escape or a way to have more things. Work can become an idol! If you are working to get a bigger house or a more expensive car or some luxury possession, then you should reevaluate your priorities. We become slaves in our pursuit to climb the success ladder.

The demands of work, family and busy schedules occupy our time. We get too busy to open the Bible and read or get on our knees and spend some precious moments with the one who died for us. But, we can turn on the television and watch an entire program. Time is something you can never make up or get back. As Christians we must learn to use our time productively and set aside time everyday to pursue God. Pursuing God should be at the top of our lists each day, second to nothing. We may have to skip or postpone an event, ballgame or meeting from time to time. We are physically tied because we eat on the run, get little exercise and are sleep deprived. We fill our schedules with nonproductive activities and ignore our responsibilities as a follower of Christ. Whatever changes we need to make to find time for God as Christians is our responsibility and is a necessity as followers of Christ.

Most Christians still attend secular movies and watch secular television. They somehow convince themselves that a little inappropriate exposure is alright. The Christian community has bought into and support movies that contain adult content and adult language with the presumption of appealing to today's generation. Secular television is broadcast right into Christian homes and watched on a regular basis. Our young children watch cartoons that depict gross and sometimes inappropriate content and language. Our teenagers are exposed to television shows that have sexual scenes that would make you blush. The commercials alone are enough to cause a Christian to become weak. This is what is going into our ears each day in our own homes. Video games and computers have replaced conversations. Texting and Facebook have become the means of communication in America. This generation even texts each other in the same car or the same house.

The Family has fallen apart with a fifty percent divorce rate and millions of children living with grandparents. The level of respect from teenagers is almost non existent. This is greatly due to fatherless and dysfunctional homes. We are reaping the evidence of children of an un-churched generation. Homes in America are filled with drugs and all kinds of perverse behaviors. This is the generation where anything is acceptable and behaviors are discussed with pride. Teenagers are proclaiming their homosexual lifestyles and having sex at an alarming young age. Drugs are commonplace in our homes and in our schools. The darkness has moved in on our communities and given us reason to be concerned for our safety.

The typical American family lives way beyond their means. They have a house that they must strive to pay the mortgage. They buy things on credit to supplement their lifestyle. This type of lifestyle also includes the Christian families. As Christians we must come to the knowledge of what is important. We live in a nation of plenty. If you have a place to live, clothes and food to eat, you are richer that two-thirds of the worlds population. How much do we need? When we leave this world we will take nothing with us except the Love in our hearts. The only things that will matter when we stand before God are the souls that you positively impacted while you lived on earth. Think about it! He won't ask what you did for a living or what kind of house you lived in or even how much money you gave to the church. He will ask "What did you do to further the Kingdom of God?" What will you say? If you have trouble answering this question, you better get busy reading His Word and finding out what it is that furthers His Kingdom.

So, is it hopeless? No, because there is a God that made it possible to come out of the darkness into the marvelous light. We still have praying parents and grandparents who diligently pray for this un-churched generation. We have prayer warriors who pray for our communities and schools. There are many success stories of people who are lead out to the darkness, people who are changed by the almighty hand of our Almighty God. Hope still exists and there is hope for every person.

"Not everyone who says to me, 'Lord, Lord,' will enter the kingdom of heaven, but the one who does the will of my Father who is in heaven. On that day many will say to me, 'Lord, Lord, did we not prophesy in your name, and cast out demons in your name, and do many mighty works in your name?' And then will I declare to them, 'I never knew you; depart from me, you workers of lawlessness" (Matthew 7:21-23)

Can you imagine that even those who did many mighty works in His name will not enter into the gates of heaven? Today's Christians need to stop thinking that once under grace always under grace. There is going to come a day when we stand before God and answer for all our sins. "For as the heaven is high above the earth, so great is His mercy toward them that fear him. As far as the east is from the west, so far hath he removed our transgressions from us" (Psalms 103:11-12). This scripture says those who FEAR Him. Fear means that we strive to do our best to live Holy lives. When we fear something or someone we try our best to do as we are told in order to escape the consequences. Christians need to adopt the philosophy of "What would Jesus do?"

Matthew 7:21-23 is clear and says that many people who call themselves Christians will not enter Heaven. This scripture alone should concern every Christian. But, there are many scriptures that plainly tell us how we are to behave. The Ten Commandments give us specific direction on what we should and should not do. And in the New Testament, the Word of God evens sums them up in two specific commands: love the Lord our God with all your heart and love you neighbor as yourself.

The only way that we can accomplish loving our neighbor as ourselves is to have the love of Jesus in our hearts. When we love Jesus, we want to please Him. When we have an intimate relationship with Him we develop a love that surpasses what we a capable of doing on our own. The Holy Spirit dwells inside us as soon as we receive salvation. I said He because the Holy Spirit is a person. He is a Spirit sent by God to be our comforter. "But the Comforter, which is the Holy Ghost, whom the Father will send in my name, he shall teach you all things to your remembrance whatsoever I have said unto you" (John 14:26).

So how do you get to a place in our walk with God that all that matters is to please Him? For we walk by faith, not by sight (2 Corinthians 5:7). We are Christians who walk by faith "For without faith, it is impossible to please God" (Hebrews 11:6). There are different degrees of faith. Faith takes the ability to wait upon the Lord. When things are going well we relax and depend upon the Lord to bless us. When things are not going well we sometimes blame the Lord. We redefine the Lord to meet our version of what we think He should be. Even though it is written that His ways are not our ways. "For my thoughts are not your thoughts, neither are your ways my ways, saith the Lord" (Isaiah 55:8).

Now faith is the substance of things hoped for, the evidence of things not seen (Hebrews 11:1). So how do we believe in something we cannot see? Believing is not exactly the same as faith. For belief to be faith, it must be based on what is certainly true. Yet Scripture gives examples of situations where belief alone is required, even commanded. Like Peter walking on the water-- don't think, act! God even requires us to believe in him when, the situation looks bad. God requires belief and trust in moments of human weakness, but faith is what makes us strong. Faith is the state of being convinced about what we hope for.

"Hope" is the word we sometimes confuse with "wish". We wish we could be rich or could get that perfect job. We all have wish lists because we are a society of insatiable wants. This is due to our inability to fill the void in our life left by our desire for our Creator. When we accept the gift of salvation and start living a Holy life our desires and wants change. We no longer want the things of the world; we are to busy thinking about the Kingdom of God and satisfying His desires. The word Hope signifies that we desire something that we anticipate will happen. Sometimes it happens just as we hoped and other times it does not happen or turns out differently than we had hoped.

So how do we develop faith? So then faith cometh by hearing and hearing by the Word of God (Romans 10:17). As Christians we should not hear with our ears but with our heart? Our heart is our Spirit Man. He directs and convicts us in every aspect of our lives. And the Lord said, If ye had faith as a grain of mustard seed, ye might say unto this sycamine tree, Be thou plucked up by the root, and be thou planted in the sea; and it should obey you (Luke 17:6). Why do we not live in the power which God gave us? The answer is simple, it is fear and doubt. We believe that it happened in the Bible and maybe even believe that it can be done today; but, we have doubt that we are capable of being used for such miracles. We believe that someone was healed; but, we have doubt that we could also be a vessel for such power. "Verily, verily, I say unto you, He that believeth on me, the works that I do shall he do also; and greater [works] than these shall he do; because I go unto my Father. And whatsoever ye shall ask in my name, that will I do, that the Father may be glorified in the Son. If ye ask anything in my name, I will do it. If ye shall love me, keep my commandments" (John 14:12-15). Did He say GREATER works? Did He say ANYTHING?

WOW! Jesus said it and we believe it so why do we not practice it? God always requires something of us when He gives us a promise. If you have faith you can... If you love me and keep my commandments you shall have... Oh, if we could just have faith enough to believe without fear or doubt how we could glorify Him.

Fear is emotion that is not from God. A young child has little fear. They will touch a hot surface or step off a high place without fear. Fear is a learned emotion. Fear is sometimes a healthy and useful emotion. We don't want to get burned or injured. But, on the other hand we don't want fear to hinder ourselves from living a productive and fruitful life. "God is greatly to be feared in the assembly of the saints, and to be had in reverence of all them that are about Him" (Psalms 89:7). The Fear of God is the only fear that should be in our Christian lives. There are twenty-eight books of the Bible that speak of fearing God. As sinners we do not fear God; but, as saints we fear Him for we have the knowledge of His blessings or curses. "I tell you, my friends, do not be afraid of those who kill the body and after that can do no more. But I will show you whom you should fear: Fear him who, after the killing of the body, has power to throw you into hell. Yes, I tell you, fear Him" (Luke 12:4-5). Fear of God is a necessity to living a Christian life; but, there is no room for doubt. Doubt hinders us from all that God has to give us. With God ALL things are possible (Mark 10:27). He does not say some things, He says ALL things!

"Ask, and it shall be given you; seek, and ye shall find; knock, and it shall be opened unto you" (Matthew 7:7). These are promises made to us from our creator. God [is] not a man, that he should lie; neither the son of man, that he should repent: hath he said, and shall he not do [it]? or hath he spoken, and shall he not make it good? (Numbers 23:19) Before you can eliminate fear and doubt completely you must develop a deep, personal relationship with Jesus. Christians must take a step beyond salvation and allow God to come into and permeate their lives.

Before a person can build a relationship they must first accept the gift of salvation. Salvation must be authentic and not emotional. The change will happen automatically and without effort. Your heart will change and the world will look and seem different. New Christians will not be exempt to the world's problems or troubles. Yea, and all that will live godly in Christ Jesus shall suffer persecution (2 Timothy 3:12).

CHAPTER 9

Now What?

When we become Christians we confess our sins and declare that we believe that Jesus died and rose again. But, even the demons in hell believe in Him and tremble. So believing is not enough; we must ask Him into our lives and turn from sinful behaviors. We must vow not only to turn away from our sins, but we must pursue Him. This means that we must surrender to His Will and allow Him to work in our lives. "And we know that all things work together for good to those that love God, to those who are the called according to his purpose" (Romans 8:28). We do not have to do this alone however, because we have received the Holy Spirit to guide us and direct our paths.

We spend our lives looking for meaning and purpose to being born. As sinners we stifle that desire until it is everything but forgotten. When we receive salvation and are drafted into the kingdom of God, we begin to ponder our purpose. Living a holy life is not easy. It takes time to build an intimate relationship with our Savior. He has knocked and we have let Him in, now what?

Our journey begins when we seek the Lord with all our heart. Firstly, we must identify what makes us a part of the kingdom of God.

Church services can evoke emotions and make us feel sad or happy. The music is playing and the preacher is evoking our emotions. We begin to squirm in your seat and get a lump in our throat. Tears sometime swell up in our eyes and we feel overwhelmed by our feelings. The preacher makes an alter call and uses words that evokes even more emotions. It seems as if we are drawn into a whirlwind and we walk to the alter based on how we feel. People are praying for us and we feel an emotion that we do not recognize.

We leave the church and wonder what happened? The feelings and emotions we were experiencing seem to flee. We do not feel that emotion any longer and resume our life and dismiss our experience. What happened? It was emotional and not spiritual. God convicts our heart not our feelings. God freely gives salvation; but, we must receive and accept what is given to us by God. When we truly receive salvation there is no doubt between the altar and the door about what happened. God happened and you know it because the Holy Spirit is there to confirm your salvation. "The Spirit itself beareth witness with our spirit, that we are the children of God" (Romans 8:16).

Churches have begun to buy into the entertainment business. Churches are now luring people in to entertain them with music that plays on the human emotion. Mega churches have sprung up all over America because they appeal to generational differences. They make it entertaining to come to church. The music and show are modeled after the world. It is the beat and resembles secular music to the extent that we cannot tell the difference. Sometimes special effects and lighting are used to attract those looking to be entertained. They set the stage and lure the people with a counterfeit worship. The lyrics to the songs have no meaning. Counterfeit worship stirs emotion, not the spirit. Stirring emotion is temporary. When the show is over so is the experience. Stirring the spirit means the heart of the listener. When the heart is stirred the experience makes an impact on lives that last long after the show is over.

Imagine for a moment that your heart has been stirred and the impact is lingering. You know that you are saved because Grace and the Holy Spirit start to work in your life. What now? How do you begin your Christian walk? Life as you knew it is about to change and you are going to welcome it with enthusiasm. The excitement will swell up in you and you will not be able to contain it. You will tell everyone or at least they will know something is different just from the joy you emit. The progress of your new found life depends on how much time you are willing to devote to pursuing a walk with Jesus. You have a passion in your heart that you cannot ignore. You find yourself thinking different and acting different. This is the time that you struggle to make sense of your experience. This is the time you want to surround yourself with others who can help you understand and nurture you in this struggle. The struggle is simple. The spirit man and the body are struggling for control. Understanding this struggle makes it easier to recognize what is happening and how to react.

There are many people in American who never grew up in the church. They have no preconceptions about religion and Christianity. Today's newfound Christian has had little to no experience with church, prayer or praise. If you fit into this population then you are among the majority. It is difficult to know just what to expect with your new found life. There are two very important places to get the answers to your questions. Fellow Christians can be helpful but there is no substitute for reading the Word and prayer. If you do not develop a desire to read the Bible or pray, then you need to reevaluate the authenticity of your experience.

The first step is to read the Holy Bible. God will open the scriptures in a way that confirms your new found life. Next, find a bible carrying, spirit filled church. Churches are many and their beliefs are similar; but, finding the one that fits you is so very vital in your walk with God. Look for a church where your spirit is stirred and you feel comfortable. Do not attach yourself to a dead, lifeless church. Visit churches in your area and beyond. Don't judge a church on one service and keep moving until you find one where you feel God has led you. You will know it in your spirit. The church will feel like home and you will be eager to attend every time the doors open. The saints will greet you with love and encourage you in your quest to grow in His kingdom. You will immediately feel a part of something bigger than yourself.

Take your time and be sure that the church you have found lines up with the Word of God. The Bible is the truth and the Holy Spirit is your guide. There are sixty-six books in the Holy Bible and all are relevant to your Christian walk. Churches who believe that certain parts of the Bible should be ignored or changed should be avoided. Be aware that there are churches that obscure the truth and teach false doctrine. Remember to match what is being preached with the Word of God. If there are discrepancies do not be deceived. "And Jesus answered and said unto them, Take heed that no man DECEIVE you" (Matthew 24:4). Not only will your walk with Jesus depend on finding a God fearing church, your very salvation may be in jeopardy. Let the Holy Spirit lead and guide you to the truth. This only comes through prayer and pursuit for the truth.

In the beginning you will not know how to pray. That is normal. You know how to talk and that is how you will begin. Just make sure you set aside time just to talk (pray). Prayer is the door that opens up access to an intimate relationship with the Lord. Sometimes you will not know what to say. This is also normal. Sometimes we need to listen and recognize His voice. Speak to Him. He is your friend and He wants to spend time with you. There will be times when you don't want to pray. Do it anyway. Listen closely! It is not about what *you* want! It does not matter in what position you pray; but, if you are able, spend some time on your knees. Praying on your knees is a way in which you can humble yourself before God. Be patient, do not get discouraged and do not compare yourself to others who use eloquent words with scripture thrown in. Developing a prayer life takes time. The important thing is you are persistent and take the time to be alone with God. In time you will be able to communicate in a way you never thought possible.

Take time to read the Bible. You cannot grow as a Christian without reading the Word. The Bible comes in different versions and translations, which can get confusing. It is written; "If any of you lack wisdom, let him ask of God, that giveth to all [men] liberally, and upbraideth not; and it shall be given him" (James 1:5). So, what version you chose is up to you. Just make sure it is the Holy Bible that has not been altered from its original content. There are new Bibles coming on the market now that have altered the scriptures in a way to reflect the new world perspective. You may want to talk to an elder of the church or pastor and get some advice; but the ultimate decision should be made through prayer. Prayer is our way of communicating with the Lord. .....the effective fervent prayer of a righteous man availeth much (James 5:16). "Do not be anxious about anything, but in everything, by prayer and petition, with thanksgiving, present your requests to God. And the peace of God, which transcends all understanding, will guard your hearts and your minds in Christ Jesus" (Philippians 4:6-7).

The Bible is our instructions on how we should live. It gives us hope, guidance and answers to all questions. Your first step to finding directions should include prayer and God's Word. Pastors and our brothers and sisters will give us encouragement, comfort and advice. Surrounding ourselves with the body of Christ (church) is a necessity for giving us strength. Remember, the church is made up of people who are human and have human characteristics. "I appeal to you, brothers, to watch out for those who cause divisions and create obstacles contrary to the doctrine that you have been taught; avoid them" (Romans 16:17). There will most likely come a time when only you can decide what God wants you to do. So, make Him your best friend and the one you turn to first in time of trouble and time of jubilation. You will find more strength and peace in Him than anywhere else.

When you seek Him you will find Him. That is God's promise and you can trust and rely on God's Word. And when you find Him your heart changes; your life is rearranged and your joy is overflowing. When you are focused on Jesus your attitude and personality change; therefore, you are set apart. Changes are apparent to those around you and your light shines everywhere you go. "Ye are the light of the world. A city that is set on the hill cannot be hid. Neither do men light a candle, and put it under a bushel, but on a candlestick, and it giveth light unto all that are in the house" (Matthew 5: 14-15).

Praise transports us into the realm of the supernatural and into the power of God. "Blessed are the people that know the joyful sound: they shall walk, O LORD, in the light of thy countenance" (Psalms 89:15). Praise should be present in the daily lives of Christians. So how do we praise Him? The Bible gives examples of specific ways to praise: Declaring of thanks (Hebrews 13:15); Clapping hands and shouting (Psalms 47:1); Musical instruments and dancing (Psalms 150:4); Singing praise songs (Psalms 9:11); Psalms, hymns, & spiritual songs (Ephesians 5:19-20); Making a joyful noise (Psalms 98:4); By lifting our hands (Psalms 134:2); By being still (Psalms 4:3-5, 46:10); and, By being loud (Psalms 33:3, 95:1-6). By him therefore let us offer the sacrifice of praise to God continually, that is, the fruit of our lips giving thanks to his name (Hebrews 13:15). How you praise is not as important as that you do praise Him.

There are hundreds of scriptures that speak of praising the Lord. "And a voice came from the throne, saying, "Give praise to our God, all you His bond-servants, you who fear Him, the small and the great." Then I heard something like the voice of a great multitude and like the sound of many waters and like the sound of mighty peals of thunder, saying, "Hallelujah! For the Lord our God, the Almighty, reigns ..." (Revelation 19:5-6). There is no doubt that there is praise in Heaven. Your kingdom come on earth as it is in Heaven. We should exalt and praise Him with the same reverence as He receives in Heaven. God is worthy to be praised! The most important part of praise to remember is that it is personal. We must be respectful not to pass judgment on others who offer praise in a different way. We are only responsible for our own relationship with God. So, always praise in spirit and in truth as you lift your praise to the one who dwells in your heart.

Praise is the most important part of your Christian life. Praise ushers in the presence of God. The music you listen to makes a big difference in your quest for spiritual growth. Praise is as important as reading the Word. Music contains words that are placed into your mind. "So then faith cometh by hearing and hearing by the Word of God" (Romans 10:17). Get yourself a variety of gospel and Christian music. Play it in your house, play it in your car, play it wherever and whenever you can. The more you saturate your mind and heart with the Word of God the more you will seek Him. What you put in your ears goes to your mind; and what goes into your mind ends up in your heart. Music can enhance your walk with the Lord. It can also hinder your walk. Those who believe that they can have one foot in heaven and one foot in the world should read God's Word. No man can serve two masters: for either he will hate the one, and love the other; or else he will hold to the one, and despise the other. Ye cannot serve God and mammon (Matthew 6:24).

There are all kinds of music, both secular and Christian. Secular music should be listened to only on rare occasions and never if the lyrics contain any inappropriate words or themes. There are Christians who believe that secular music is just entertainment. Listening to secular music will place words and thoughts in your mind that will evoke the flesh. Don't be fooled into thinking that the new wave Christian music is any better. If you cannot hear the lyrics or the lyrics are not biblical or obscured, steer clear. If the music does not stir your spirit then it is not what you want to be putting into your ears. Just do a simple test: would Jesus listen or would He turn away?

The lyrics to today's Christian music, are so much like secular music that you cannot seem to distinguish the difference. Music that has lyrics that are difficult or impossible to understand is nothing more than counterfeit. Satan is the master of counterfeit. Read the lyrics of these songs that this younger generation is placing in their minds. Yes, they do mention Jesus and maybe even a line or two of coherent lyric; but, they also have lines that are obscene and demonic. Christians who continue to listen to this type of music place negative thoughts in their minds. "Finally, brethren, whatsoever things are true, whatsoever things *are* honest, whatsoever things *are* just, whatsoever things *are* pure, whatsoever things *are* lovely, whatsoever things *are* of good report; if *there be* any virtue, and if *there be* any praise, think on these things" (Philippians 4:8).

CHAPTER 10

From Milk to Meat

Anew Christian needs all the nourishment they can get to enable them to become mature Christians. The Bible states, "I have fed you with milk, and not with meat: for hitherto ye were not able to bear it, neither yet now are ye able" (1 Corinthians 3:2). For every one that useth milk is unskillful in the word or righteousness: for he is a babe. But strong meat belongeth to them that are of full age, even those who by reason of use have their senses exercised to discern both good and evil (Hebrews 5:13-14).

When we are babies we are given milk and no solid food. We have no teeth and our digestive system were not developed enough to have solid food. Can you imagine trying to give a hamburger to a two month old baby? Of course not! Babies drink milk and are helpless. This is why to survive they must have a caretaker. It is no different for a new Christian. God is the caretaker for the new Christian. He sends the Holy Spirit to guide us. And He pampers us with His gentle hands. Just look at a new Christian and you will see that their needs are met and their desires are fulfilled. Talk to a new Christian and they will talk about Jesus and what He has done and is doing in their lives. They are the first to stand up in church and proclaim His greatness.

There are Christians who never graduate from this state. Can you imagine a ten year old child who still drinks a bottle and not eating solid food? First of all they would not get the nutrients they need to develop. They would probably be frail, sick or maybe even die. This is the same for a Christian. The Word of God, Worship and the support of a church family are all spiritual meat to the new Christian. Failure to absorb the Word will make us weak and vulnerable to attack from the adversary. Have you ever wondered why Christians have so many problems? It is because they are weak. Weakness comes from isolating yourself from the Word and prayer. Strength comes from an intimate relationship with God and occasional prayer and reading the Bible puts us in a weak condition. Weakness can cause all kinds of havoc in your life. Remember "Be sober, be vigilant; because your adversary the devil, as a roaring lion, walketh about, seeking whom he may devour." (1 Peter 5:8).

Now, you may have friends whom you hung out with as a sinner and they just did not disappear. These friendships can be dangerous and should be continued with caution. Firstly, you should never place yourself in a compromising situation. You are a new creature in Christ and need to make sure your friends are aware of your new life. If these previous relationships are real they will stand the test of time. They will respect your values and either come to the truth or fall away. Either way you must not continue to socialize with friends who continue to pursue the desires of the world.

Attending church regularly is a must. "Not forsaking the assembling of ourselves together, as the manner of some is; but exhorting one another; and so much the more as ye see the day approaching" (Hebrews 10:25). We become stronger when we yoke ourselves with fellow Christians. "Be ye not unequally yoked together with unbelievers: for what fellowship hath righteousness with unrighteousness? And what communion hath light with darkness?" (2 Corinthians 6:14) Yoking yourself with fellow Christians regularly gives you strength to persevere through bad times. Spending too much time in the presence of sinners or lukewarm Christians can drain a Christian who seeks to walk in the Spirit. Assembling with those who have a hunger and desire to pursue all that God has to offer is a must. Lack of assembly with fellow believers will stunt your growth and leave you in infancy.

It is extremely important that a Christian gather with other Christians in an effort to develop. We get strength from testimonies and the light that shines through others who can give us meat. We should get excited when it is time to go to the house of the Lord. We should take the attitude of David when he said, "I was glad when they said unto me, Les us go into the house of the Lord" (Psalms 122:1). If excitement does not swell up in you when it is time to attend church, then you need to seek an answer. Maybe you need to spend more time in the Word. Maybe you need to spend more time in prayer or praise. Or, maybe you need to attend another church. I know we get comfortable and sometimes feel a loyalty to the church we grew up in or have attended for a time.

We should not be in love with a church. We should be in love with Jesus.

Churches in America are on every street corner. The signs out front display denominational connections and sometimes are nondenominational. The people assemble to lift each other up, praise God and hear a Word from God. This is not your normal church and if you find it hold onto it and continue to shine your light upon it. In the normal American church people certainly assemble and on occasion lift one another up. There is praise of some sort happening and the Word of God is usually spoken by someone in the pulpit. The truth is many churches across America have bought into some form of Christianity that has no resemblances to the first church. The Spirit has long left the people and the church. The power is not even sought and complaisant congregations go through routines or religious activities each week satisfied with their obligation.

There are now churches appearing across this nation that tolerate and sometimes proclaim blatant abominations to occur in the church. Such instances include members who are living together outside the institution of marriage and homosexual couples. There are also churches that overlook and sometimes cover up such things as molestation and extra marital affairs among their members. There is a place in the pews for people who practice such abominations; but, it is not as a member of the church. Churches should never practice discrimination; after all the purpose of the church is to win souls. All should be welcome to enter the doors of the Father's house; but, they should never be allowed to become a member until they repent and turn away from such behaviors. It is time that the Church stand up for the Holy Word of God and not water it down with the world's perception of what is acceptable. The church should be a refuge from the world instead of an extension of the world.

The "normal" church in America is just like the normal Christian. There are hindrances and hypocrites in every church. Don't be surprised and certainly do not let that discourage you from attending church. Remember we do not serve a church, we serve God. Churches will close, preachers will fall, saints will disappoint and services will leave you empty; but, God will never leave you or falter or disappoint and He will always fill the empty void. The church is not just a building; you are the church.

The purpose of the church is not to entertain or make you feel anything you haven't brought with you. Christians should prepare themselves for worship through prayer and praise prior to going through the church doors. We should put all other problems or disagreements away and focus on Him before we attend a service. Remember we are going to our Father's house and He is going to be so glad to see us.

God wants us to grow continually in our Christian walk. Don't settle for the world's definition of a Christian. Search the scriptures and obtain the knowledge you need to live an abundant life. God has gifts for those who love and diligently seek Him. Just always remember what it was like when you first became a child of God. You felt like a child who sought after your Father's attention. Keep that child attitude and enthusiasm and add to it knowledge and a hunger for more. "As for me, I will behold thy face in righteousness: I shall be satisfied, when I awake, with thy likeness" (Psalms 17:15).

In order to leave the milk and eat meat you must adhere to an intimate relationship with Jesus. You must pursue Him through prayer, praise and purpose. When you spend most of your hours thinking, talking, walking, chasing and serving God you will graduate to solid food. Don't become a Christian who is satisfied with just milk because you will never withstand the test of time and fall victim to the world. You will become just another Christian who sold out to the world or even worse a lukewarm Christian. The Word is clear on what happens to lukewarm Christians. "So then because thou art lukewarm, and neither cold nor hot, I will spew thee out of my mouth" (Revelations 3:16).

"Jesus said unto him, Thou shalt love the Lord thy God with all thy heart, and with all thy soul, and with all thy mind. This is the first and great commandment" (Matthew 22:37-38). When you find the Lord you will love Him and your neighbor because your heart and spirit will command it. The Love will envelop you like a warm blanket and you will experience a peace. Be careful for nothing; but in everything by prayer and supplication with thanksgiving let your requests be made known unto God. And the peace of God, which passeth all understanding, shall keep your hearts and minds through Christ Jesus (Philippians 4:6-7).

CHAPTER 11

Wait

We all experience a period in our Christian life where we do not get instant answers to our prayers. We must realize that our time is not His time. It is difficult to know what God wants us to do. We must show our trust in Him by waiting upon the Lord. "But they that wait upon the LORD shall renew their strength; they shall mount up with wings as eagles; they shall run, and not be weary; and they shall walk, and not faint" (Isaiah 40:31). When we make decisions on our own they can have devastating results.

Obedience is a must for Christians who wish to live a life in God's favor. Our relationship with God should be personal. To understand we could compare our relationship with God to our relationship with our children or someone we love. When we love someone we want to make them happy. We can't make them happy all the time because sometimes we disagree with them on certain issues. Take for instance, your three-year old comes and says they want to go out and play in the rain. It is thundering and lightening and you say, "no". The child does not understand and cries and tries to get you to change your mind. You are not going to change your mind because what they ask is dangerous. As a loving parent you try to explain to the child the danger of going out when it is lightening. The child is so busy crying and doesn't hear you. You must wait until they are quite and try again to explain. This is exactly the way God deals with His children. We must sometimes take time to listen to what God is trying to do and spend quite time with Him.

On the other hand, God loves His children so much that if we insist on doing it our way, then He will let us have our way. For example, your teenager comes to you and wants to go to a party and you know the party will not be chaperoned. You say "no" and explain the dangers of attending such a party. Your teenager gets angry and tries to change your mind. You stick to your original answer of "no". The night of the party comes and the teenager sneaks out and goes to the party anyway. The teenager participates in drinking and inappropriate behavior. You tried to protect them and explained the danger; but, they chose to do it without your permission.

Our relationship with God must consist of a two-way dialogue. When we are standing in the valley of decision and God does not give us an answer, we must wait. We humans are not good at waiting. We want instant gratification. We live busy lives and expect things to be convenient. The world is becoming a place where waiting is a thing of the past.

Let's look at inventions that have made us a society that can't wait. Microwaves cook our food in minutes, drive-thrus give us our food in minutes, DVR's and television on demand allows us to watch at our convenience. We have drive-through pharmacies and even drive-through chapels. The Internet gives us answers almost instantly, anywhere at anytime. Cell phones allow us to have conversations without the wasted time of talking. Busy signals are gone due to call-waiting. The days of waiting in lines are almost non-existent because we can accomplish so much of our business online. Stores now have self-check out to keep us from waiting. Everything moves fast so being patient is becoming obsolete.

Most people want an instant answer to questions. We live a busy life and when we have to wait we feel frustrated. The result of impatience is road-rage, arguments, anger, stress and loss of self control. We have become a society who expects quick results. Because of our "right now" mentality waiting is difficult. There was a time when you had no choice but to wait. Cakes were baked in ovens and then have to cool to be iced. Stores were closed on Sunday. There were not any drive-thrus for anything. We had to wait for the mail to come. We had to wait until our parents stopped talking before we were allowed to speak.

Waiting or patience, is almost non-existent in the US culture today. As Christians, learning to wait upon an answer is our hardest lesson. Seems the older we are the more patience we possess. Patience must be important to God because He addressed it numerous times in the Bible. Christians should possess the fruits of the Spirit. "But the fruit of the Spirit is love, joy, peace, **long –suffering** (patience), gentleness, goodness, faith," (Galatians 5:22). It is not easy to wait on the Lord; but, as Christians we must learn to because His time is not our time. We must learn to trust Him and wait. By making us wait God promises that He will renew our strength and we will not grow weary.

Troubles will come because we live in this world and we are not immune to adversity. "We are troubled on every side, yet not distressed; we are perplexed, but not in despair; Persecuted, but not forsaken; cast down, but not destroyed;" (2 Corinthians 4:8-9). It is how we react and handle troubles that shows our trust in the Lord. What do we do when trouble comes? Do we expect God to take it or do we go to God and discuss it? Christians should take their petition to the Lord and trust that He will answer in His time. "And if we know that He hears us, whatever we ask, we know that we have the petitions that we have asked of Him" (1 John 5:15).

God is faithful to keep His promises. "Know therefore that the LORD thy God, he *is* God, the faithful God, which keepeth covenant and mercy with them that love him and keep his commandments to a thousand generations" (Deuteronomy 7:9). That should give us encouragement to know that to a thousand generations He will stay faithful to keep His promises.

Christians need to realize that waiting can be extremely pleasurable. When God does not give us an instant answer to our problem or plea, we must know that God has a reason. Let's look at the scriptures and look at what we know for sure. In Jeremiah 29:11 He said, "For I know the plans I have for you," declares the LORD, "plans to prosper you and not to harm you, plans to give you hope and a future". This sounds like His plans are to give us success. Well that sounds like His plans are to make our life better. God's answers and help always come just at the right time. All we have to do is put our trust in Him and know that we are safe in

His hands. Who shall separate us from the love of Christ? *shall* tribulation, or distress, or persecution, or famine, or nakedness, or peril, or sword? (Romans 8:35)

The most difficult time is when you do not know what to do in times of crisis. Well thanks to the Bible Christians know what to do. He gives us specific instructions for every situation. The reason we don't know what to do is because we have not read the instructions. Another explanation for confusion is that we read it but we forget. If this is the case, we need to read it again and place it in our hearts. The last explanation for confusion is that we just don't believe it. This is when we need to go back to the beginning and ask ourselves why? We proclaim that we are Christians and claim that we believe in the Bible.

So, why do many Christians not see answers to their prayers? There are several explanation for unanswered prayer. "Ye ask, and receive not, because ye **ask amiss**, that ye may consume *it* upon your lusts" (James 4:3). Sometimes our prayers are for things that are not good for us. God knows our intentions even when we do not. "And all things, whatsoever ye shall ask in prayer, **believing**, ye shall receive" (Matthew 21:22). When we pray we must believe that what we are praying for will manifest. "And this is the confidence that we have in him, that, if we ask any thing **according to his will**, he heareth us: And if we know that he hear us, whatsoever we ask, we know that we have the petitions that we desired of him"(1 John 5:14-15). It could not be clearer. If we pray according to His will believing and our intentions are for the good, then God will generously deliver.

Wait for the Lord; Be strong, and let your heart take courage; Yes, wait for the Lord" (Psalms 27:14). It is not easy to wait up on the Lord. Christians must rely upon their relationship with God. "I am the good shepherd; I know my sheep and my sheep know me" (John 10:14). We must learn to know the voice of God and the peace that comes from listening and obeying. Our time is not His time; but, His time is just in time. So wait on Him to direct your steps and you will never be disappointed.

CHAPTER 12

The Quest

W hat is the truth? To find that out we have to take a journey. We have to assess our lives and figure out what really makes us happy. Think about a happy memory you had as a child. Chances are it involved someone who cared enough about you to place that memory in your mind. Happy childhood memories are usually simply feeling important and loved. We don't ask much as a child just to feel safe and loved. Now think of a happy memory as a teenager. That is a tough one! Again it probably involved someone who you respected and took the time to notice you in some way. Our wants are a little different as a teenager; but, acceptance and compassion usually make our list as happy memories.

Now, think about as an adult what makes us happy. Was it a time when you where with a friend or a relative you loved and loved you? Was your joy due to the acceptance or compassion you felt from someone special? These are emotions that the soul yearns for and only finds on occasion. What if you could find that joy everyday, in every aspect of your life? No matter what your circumstances you could feel that same joy you felt in the your most happy moments.

WOW! That could be worth the journey. Well there is a way, if you are willing to give up everything the world has to offer. You must still live here; but, you must hate the ways of the world. "Love not the world, neither the things *that are* in the world. If any man love the world, the love of the Father is not in him. For all that *is* in the world, the lust of the flesh, and the lust of the eyes, and the pride of life, is not of the Father, but is of the world" (1 John 2: 15-16).

What does this mean? It means that anything that is not productive for survival or to advance the Kingdom of God must go. You must spend more hours of your day advancing the Kingdom than you do working, eating or sleeping. Most of us work to survive and support our families. Ok, how many hours do you have to work to really support your family? I am not talking about supporting them in the way the world has grown accustomed too; but, supporting them in a way that advances the Kingdom of God. Next, how much time do you spend eating? Do you eat properly? Do you eat with your family or others? What kind of conversations do you have over meals? What about sleeping? Do you get enough or too much? This is a lot to think about; but, to begin this journey you are going to need a journal.

The success of this journal depends on how much time you are willing to devote to be happy and advancing the Kingdom of God. It is a journey that will open your eyes and ears to things you have never experienced but have yearned for all your life. By keeping a journal that emptiness will not only be filled, but it will be emptied and refilled many times. The journey I am speaking of is the quest for the Glory of God. Many have chased it, some have seen it and few have experienced it. How bad do you want it? Do you want it so bad that your soul yearns for it? Do you want it so bad that nothing else matters? Do you want it so bad that you think you shall surely perish without it? If you answered yes to these questions, then continue on your journey to find an extraordinary experience. There is no requirement for you to take such a journey. If you are satisfied with your ordinary Christian life, God has made a way. "Verily, verily, I say unto you, He that believeth on me hath everlasting life (John 7:1).

The first thing you need to do is write down how you spend your time. This means every hour of every day for one week. Be honest and record as you go through your day. Don't wait till the end of the day and try to remember how you spent your day. A recorder would help and give you the freedom to make a more adequate account of your time. Once you have successfully accounted for every hour for a week, then find some quiet time and evaluate the results. Make yourself two columns one headed Kingdom, the other headed World. Since many of us have a job and must work to survive, most of our work day could be placed under the Kingdom. "Whatever you do, work at it with all your heart, as working for the Lord, not for men" (Colossians 3:23). But, to place your working hours under the Kingdom column, you must evaluate each hour and ask yourself the question "Did I do my job as if I were working for the Lord?"

Next, carefully go through your days and place under the Kingdom column anything that you did that advanced the Kingdom of God. This could be as simple as a kind word or gesture or as great as leading someone to salvation. It includes the obvious reading the Bible, prayer, and witnessing; but could also include a conversation about the Lord. Advancing the Kingdom of God is anything you did that was in line with the Word of God.

In the other column headed World, put anything you did that involved participating in the world. All the following could be placed under this column: idle conversations, watching secular television or listening to secular music, listening to or participating in any activity that does not line up with the Word of God. When you are finished you should have somewhere around 112 hours. That allows for approximately eight hours of sleep. Remember to count anytime you awaken during the night and how you spend that time.

Finally, add up the hours during the week where you advanced the kingdom of God and the hours which you conformed to the world. Did you spend most of your hours advancing the Kingdom? If you are a Christian, you should have listed going to church under the Kingdom heading. Now, think about what you did in church. Did you glorify God during that time? Did you worship Him in spirit and in truth? Did you listen intently to the message? Did you go for yourself or for Him? This kind of thinking makes us evaluate our motives and that is sometimes difficult.

Why do we go to church? Be honest. Is going to church exciting or a chore? Do we go to check it off our Christian obligation or because we love our Father? Do we go to be entertained or to lift up our creator? Is it to receive or to give? Tough questions and the answers could surprise you. Does it make you a bad Christian if the answers were not what you expected? No, because most Christian don't even think about the answers to such questions.

But, to get closer and experience the Glory these questions are necessary.

Are you ready to experience what God wants in your life? When you have had the time to analyze your journal, make sure you take the time to pray and ask God to guide you to the truth. Once you have completed your analysis, ask yourself, "Am I desperate for Jesus? Am I willing to pay the price and be set apart?" Because, you *are* going to be different! Your view of the world will be changed! Your relationships with the ones you love may even be different. "Anyone who loves his father or mother more than me is not worthy of me; anyone who loves his son or daughter more than me is not worthy of me; (Matthew 10:37). This is difficult and you may be tested on this scripture. Just know that God has a plan and His plan is the best plan. "For I know the plans I have for you, declares the LORD, plans for welfare and not for evil, to give you a future and a hope" (Jeremiah 29:11). So, to fulfill the plans which God has for us we must trust in His Word.

Are you willing to put all your trust in Him and surrender to His Will, to His Ways? Most people stop short of His Glory. Why, because it takes sacrifice and effort. I believe that God calls us all to salvation. I believe His Word "For many are called, but few *are* chosen. (Matthew 22:15). Those who have a hunger and pursue the face of God are the chosen. They thirst after righteousness "Blessed are they which do hunger and thirst after righteousness: for they shall be filled" (Matthew 5:6). The chosen find it joy in the fact that they are set apart. "Blessed are they which are persecuted for righteousness' sake: for theirs is the kingdom of heaven. Blessed are ye, when men shall revile you, and persecute you, and shall say all manner of evil against you falsely, for my sake. Rejoice, and be exceeding glad: for great is your reward in heaven: for so persecuted they the prophets which were before you (Matthew 5: 10-12).

You decide, are you called or chosen? Either way you will go to heaven and have eternal life; but, if you are chosen you are never satisfied. The yearning does not go away and you are always seeking a deeper relationship with God. You are anxiously awaiting His return. You want and seek to experience the fullness of God. Remember few are chosen and if you feel this way you are not alone and you are not crazy. There are others who are drawn by the same spirit. A spirit who seeks to be one with the Savior, who finds it gain to sacrifice everything to be in His presence. The journey will be worth the reward. "Now there is in store for me the crown of righteousness, which the Lord, the righteous Judge, will award to me on that day--and not only to me, but also to all who have longed for his appearing" (2 Timothy 4:8).

If you chose to follow the path of righteousness, know that the road can be rough. Know that you do not have to do anything alone. "Trust in the LORD with all thine heart; and lean not unto thine own understanding" (Proverbs 3:5). Take life one day at a time and believe that God is with you even when you fall. The Word is your weapon learn it and make it part of your daily conversations. It is important that you pray for yourself as well as well as others.

Some people believe that praying for yourself is selfish. "And it is my prayer that your love may abound more and more, with knowledge and all discernment, so that you may approve what is excellent, and so be pure and blameless for the day of Christ, filled with the fruit of righteousness that comes through Jesus Christ, to the glory and praise of God" (Philippians 1:9-11). This sounds like a personal prayer to me. Our quest will never end until we shed these mortal bodies and are transformed into our glorified bodies.

CHAPTER 13

Revival

In the Christian community we speak of revival. Those who experience it are changed forever and become a witness to its power. Christians travel the nation and sometimes the world seeking it. Sometime seekers come back rejuvenated and ready to light a fire in their own churches. They have been in the presence of God and found the power of God at work. The scriptures describe it – "And when the day of Pentecost was fully come, they were all with one accord in one place. And suddenly there came a sound from heaven as of a rushing mighty wind and it filled all the house where they were sitting. And there appeared unto them cloven tongues like as of fire, and it sat upon each of them and they were all filled with the Holy Ghost; and began to speak with other tongues; as the spirit gave them utterance." (Acts 2:1-4). This was the first revival.

There are miraculous miracles happening all over the world and most of us dismiss it as not real or unattainable. Some Christians even believe that Pentecost was just a one-time incident and couldn't happen today. Jesus Christ is the same yesterday, today and forever (Hebrews 13:8). So if Jesus did it as it is written then why do we not seek the same? Is it because we lack faith? Surely the Christian has the faith of a mustard seed. Is it because we do not believe what the Bible says? We are Christians who base our whole lives on the Word of God. Is it because we have doubt? That is close because doubt does hinder us from receiving the gifts which God wants to give us. The thief cometh not, but for to steal, and to kill, and to destroy; I am come that they might have life, and that they might have it more abundantly (John 10:10).

Some Christians believe that the Old Testament is to be ignored. It is just an assortment of stories and does not apply to us today. How can Christians explain Jesus' words in Matthew? "Think not that I am come to destroy the law, or the prophets; I am not come to destroy, but to fulfill. For verily I say unto you, Till heaven and earth pass, one jot or one tittle shall in no way pass from the law, till all be fulfilled" (Matthew 5:17-18). Heaven and earth has not passed away and prophecy has not been fulfilled. These are the words of Jesus; Hello!

Each person should ask themselves if they are a fan or follower of Christ. Sunday mornings seem to be when churches have their largest attendance. So what happens to people on Sunday nights or Wednesday night prayer meetings? Some churches have succumbed to just having one service on Sundays due to poor attendance. Most all Christians will say they are a follower. But, a follower means you want to be like the person you are following. Sacrifice must be made when you want to be a follower. When we follow our dream we will sacrifice time, money and sometimes relationships. We spend most of our time engaged in activities that will make that dream a reality. What are you willing to sacrifice to be a follower of Jesus Christ? He won't settle for part of you. And regardless of what some may say you can't take it too far!

Do you want to live the abundant life? Sure you do! "If ye then, being evil, know how to give good gifts unto your children: how much more shall your heavenly Father give the Holy Spirit to those who ask Him" (Luke 11:13). Jesus said, ..." if any man will come after me, let him deny himself, and take up his cross daily and follow me. For whosoever will save his life shall lose it: but whoever will lose his life for my sake, the same shall save it. (Luke 9:23-24) This sounds so simple, doesn't it? The problem is we have to do something to receive the power and the gifts that God has for us. Gifts, that sounded great. Hold on, He said "deny ourselves, take up our cross DAILY"! And then He goes on to say "lose our lives"! This is just exactly what He wants from us and it is possible to do this with joy and eagerness. This is called sacrifice and no one sacrificed as much as our Lord, Jesus Christ.

Revival starts with one person eager to please the Lord. That person begins to have a relationship with Jesus. Alone a person seeks Him with a passion and pursues Him until they find Him. They enter His presence and find refuge from the world. Then, they find rest in His arms and visit often. The relationship becomes personal and more intimate. They hunger for Him and yearn for Him and find themselves in a place where words are not enough. The Glory surrounds them and engulfs them with Peace and an overwhelming Love. An experience such as this will bring you into a new realm. You will be so filled that you will overflow and need to get refilled. You find yourself desiring to experience this over and over again. This is individual revival! You start wanting other people to join you in this place of refuge and Love. This is when and where revival is born.

Revival starts when a group of people are individually in love with our Savior Jesus Christ. A Christian can have an individual revival and walk alone for a while basking in the light of His presence. And one person can stir a desire in others that could unite a revival. Oh, but when a group of people assemble and all have been basking, look out! God will show up in a mighty way. The scriptures say we must deny ourselves. What does that mean? To deny is to refuse to admit the truth or existence.

All human beings have a body and a soul. When we become a Christian the Father sends us the Holy Spirit to reside in us. Our body is sin and the Holy Spirit is perfect with no sin. So what about our soul? Well our body (flesh) and our Spirit fight for control of our soul. When we sin our body wins, when we are blameless our Spirit wins. Our goal as Christians is to walk in the Spirit. "This I say then, Walk in the Spirit, and ye shall not fulfill the lust of the flesh" (Galatians 5:16).

To deny ourselves means to walk in the Spirit. How can we overcome the desires of the flesh? First we have to identify what the desires are. What does the body crave that we can deny? The body craves many things. It is different for each of us; but, one thing we all crave is food. This is a necessity for survival; although, we can deny it for a period of time. There are many scripture both in the Old and New Testament that talk about fasting. Although it is a personal decision, it is a sacrifice to deepen your relationship with God and must have a purpose. Prayer must accompany a fast or it is done in vain.

Fasting is only one way to deny ourselves. Our flesh is sin; so, cleansing ourselves from anything that is blocking our quest for a closer relationship with God is denying our flesh. Anytime the Spirit leads us to do something and we just don't want to and we do it anyway we deny the flesh. Denying the flesh builds strength and faith in our ability to live a Christian life. "For they that are after the flesh; do mind the things of the flesh; but they that are after the Spirit the things of the Spirit" (Romans 8:5). Whatever you are spending your time thinking about determines who is under control. If you spend most of your time thinking about God and godly things then you are walking in the Spirit. If you spend most of your time thinking about worldly things then you are walking in the flesh. "…Whatsoever things are true, whatsoever things are honest, whatsoever things are just, whatsoever things are pure, whatsoever things are lovely, whatsoever things are of good report; if there be any virtue and if there be any praise, think these things (Philippians 4:8).

The time has come when Christians must grow up and eat the meat and mature into Christians who are useful in the kingdom of God. "No man can serve two masters; for either he will hate the one, and love the other; or else he will hold to the one, and despise the other. Ye cannot serve God and mammon" (Matthew 6: 24). If you are holding onto something in the world that contradicts the Word of God then you are not serving God you are serving the world. We should put NOTHING before him. No man knows when Jesus will return in His glory to rapture the church. "But of that day and hour knoweth no man, no, not the angels in heaven, but my Father only" (Matthew 24:36). Even though we do not know the exact day, we do know the signs of the coming of the Lord.

There are six signs given by Jesus that indicates the end of the age. "For many will come in my name, saying, I am Christ, and will mislead many." (Matthew 24:5) "And many false prophets will arise, and will mislead many." (Matthew 24:11) There have been many false prophets and they pop up every day leading people to believe false doctrine and sometimes even leading them to mass suicides. "And you will be hearing of wars and rumors of wars; see that you are not frightened, for those things must take place, but that is not yet the end." (Matthew 24:6) "For nation will rise against nation, and kingdom against kingdom and in various places there will be famines and earthquakes." (Matthew 24:7) All you have to do is watch the world news or track this on the Internet and find that this is happening right now.

"But all these things are merely the beginning of birth pangs. Then they will deliver you to tribulation, and will kill you, and you will be hated by all nations on account of my name." (Matthew 24:8-9). Christians around the world are being martyred every day for their belief in Jesus Christ. America is a nation that is mainly protected from persecution; but everyday Christians in this country are hated and ridiculed for their beliefs. "And this gospel of the kingdom shall be preached in the whole world for a witness to all the nations, and then the end shall come." (Matthew 24:14) These things have already come to pass. ALL these things! There is nothing more that must happen before the rapture of the church.

The apostle Paul also wrote about the end times. "But realize this, that in the last days difficult times will come. For men will be lovers of self, lovers of money, boastful, arrogant, disobedient to their parents, ungrateful, unholy, unloving, unforgiving, malicious gossips, without self-control, brutal, haters of good, treacherous, reckless, conceited, lovers of pleasure rather than lovers of God; holding to a form of godliness, although they have denied its power; always learning and never able to come to the knowledge of the truth." (2 Timothy 3:1-5, 7) "But the spirit explicitly says that in later times some will fall away from the faith, paying attention to deceitful spirits and doctrines of demons. By means of the hypocrisy of liars seared in their own conscience as with a branding iron, men who forbid marriage and advocate abstaining from foods which God has created to be gratefully shared in by those who believe and know the truth." (I Timothy 4:1-3) All you have to do is look around and see that all these things are happening everyday. Turn on the news and turmoil that our world is in and compare it with the scriptures and there is no denying that we are in the last days. The rapture of church could be any day.

God did not want us to be unprepared. He gave us specific signs to warn us of the coming of the Lord. His hope is that we all come to realize that the end is near. He Loves us and wants us to have ever lasting life. He calls us and gives us every opportunity to accept Him as our Savior. It is up to every individual person whether sinner or saint to make his or her own decision to accept or reject the Word of God. One thing is for sure; sinners will perish and find themselves in the darkness that they chose. Christians who think they can hold onto the world and enter Heaven are going to also find themselves in darkness.

The population of the world is about seven billion. "For the gate is wide and the way is easy that leads to destruction, and those who enter by it are many. For the gate is narrow and the way is hard that leads to life, and those who find it are few" (Matthew 7:13-14). Oh, those Christians who seek God and live to follow His will wake up someday in the light of His Glory. We don't know when. We don't know if it will be in the rapture or when we are called home; but, we know for sure that we will experience the Glory.

What about now? What about in the meantime while we still walk the earth? Are we seeking Him with all we have or are we giving Him what is left over? Are you one of those people who seek revival and willing to sacrifice your time, energy, finances and even your life to see it happen? It won't be easy and there is no room for fear or doubt. Living in the peace and arms of The God Almighty will be more than enough to sustain you and place you right in the middle of a revival.

What are the steps you must take to experience real authentic revival? It is simple, we have instructions. We have had these instructions all our lives. It is called the Holy Bible. Read it, believe it, live it. Find yourself a bible carrying, Holy Ghost filled church and do your part to start a fire.

CHAPTER 14

Eternal Life

Our body is a temporary vessel born in sin and desires to sin. Every human has a soul that occupies their body. The soul has always existed and always will exist. The soul is what some people may call that little voice that distinguishes between right and wrong. Most everyone will admit they have a little internal voice which has caused them to make the right decision and not listening to that voice has caused them to make the wrong decision. The soul and Spirit are two separate entities. Every human does not possess a spirit. The spirit or the Holy Spirit is only possessed by those who have accepted the gift of salvation. The Holy Spirit is a gift from God and is Holy and without sin. It cannot continue to live in a person who continually and purposely sins. The gift of salvation is free and possible because Jesus Christ died on the cross.

Now that we know that we have a body (sin), a soul (neutral) and a Spirit (Holy and without sin) we must understand the battle that rages in every born again Christian. When you accept the gift of salvation, the Holy Spirit and the body fight to control your soul. Remember your soul is neutral and it will be subject to be controlled by either the body or Spirit. If you give into sin then the body controls your soul; but, if you are obedient to the will of God and keep His commandments the Holy Spirit controls your soul. The more you surrender to the Holy Spirit the stronger and closer you get to an intimate relationship with God. The more you give into the desires of the flesh (body) the more you will distance yourself from your Savior. Eventually sin will cause you to fall back into your destructive sinful life.

When we receive salvation, the Holy Spirit comes into our body and convicts, helps and comforts us. He desires to become prominent in our lives and strives to help us become holy. This is what it means to walk in the Spirit. We can never be perfect and sin will always be a part of our lives because we must live in these bodies while we live on this earth. To what degree we surrender to the body (sin) is up to each of us. We can strive to get our flesh under submission by adhering to the Word of God.

The more knowledge we have the better equipped we will be for the battle. It is a battle that rages in every born-again Christian. Knowledge is power and without knowledge you will be defenseless against the forces that you will eventually encounter. "Wherefore take unto you the whole armor of God that ye may be able to withstand in the evil day, and having done all, to stand. Stand therefore, having your loins girt about with truth, and having on the breastplate of righteousness; And your feet shod with the preparation of the gospel of peace; Above all, taking the shield of faith, wherewith ye shall be able to quench all the fiery darts of the wicked. And take the helmet of salvation, and the sword of the Spirit, which is the word of God: Praying always with all prayer and supplication in the Spirit, and watching thereunto with all perseverance and supplication for all saints;" (Ephesians 6:13-18).

Each born again Christian must make the decision on how he or she will spend their day on this earth. I say "day" because none of us is promised tomorrow. If this were your last day, what would you do? It may very well be your last day. What have you done today to advance the kingdom that you could tell your creator when you stand face to face? Have you used or displayed the gifts of the Spirit? Have you let your light shine? Have you proclaimed His name? Have you prayed? Have you read His Word? If you answered no to these questions, you need hope this is not your last day. These are the basic daily things every Christian must do naturally without excuse or exception. Not *should do* or *may do*, but *must do*!

There is coming a day when we will leave this world and our soul will ascend from our earthly bodies and will either go to heaven or hell. The days of living in bondage blinded by the master of deceit is coming to an end. Satan's time is short and he is becoming desperate to keep the blinders on the children of light. Hell is a very real place and meant for Satan and his demons. It is filled with darkness, loneliness and eternal fire. In the King James Bible, "hell" is used 54 times; 31 times in the Old Testament, and 23 times in the New Testament.

Heaven is also a real place and it is filled with love and peace that surpasses our understanding. Think of a time in your life when you were happy. Think of the feeling you felt and magnify it ten million times and that will not even compare to what God has in store for those who love and obey Him. "But as it is written, Eye hath not seen, nor ear heard, neither have entered into the heart of man, the things which God hath prepared for them that love him" (1 Corinthians 2:9).

Eternal life is a promise given by God to those who accept the gift of salvation. "For I am persuaded, that neither death, nor life, nor angels, nor principalities, nor powers, nor things present, nor things to come, nor height, nor depth, nor any other creature, shall be able to separate us from the love of God, which is in Christ Jesus our Lord" (Romans 8:38-39).

I was once in a Sunday school class and we were talking about salvation. One of my fellow Christians made the statement: "when we accept the gift of salvation, then we could set in a chair for the rest of our lives and still go to Heaven". This bothered me for the longest time. I was a new Christian and wondered how could someone accept the gift of salvation and not share it with others. Throughout the scriptures it is written that God seeks to bless His children. As children of God we must be willing to believe His Word and obey His commands.

If we accept the gift of salvation, then we are also given the desire to seek a relationship with our Creator. God did not give us the gift of salvation and then leave us to ourselves. "For the scripture saith, whosoever believeth on him shall not be ashamed (Romans 10:11). The gift of salvation comes with a desire to serve Him and proclaim Him as our Savior. Just setting and doing nothing is not salvation; it is a deception created by the counterfeiter. Search the scriptures; for in them ye think ye have eternal life: and they are they which testify of me (John 5:39).

Someday I will stand before Him in His marvelous light. I will fall to my knees or my face and He will lift me up and I will look upon His face. The one who saved me by His grace and He will take me by the hand and lead me through the promise land. What a wonderful day that will be. Until that time I will diligently work for my Lord by shining my light. I will not hide my light nor be ashamed of proclaiming the Gospel of Jesus Christ. He died on the cross for you and me and now sets on the right side of God.

I am eternally grateful that He has chosen me at such a time as this. I will serve Him and live for Him until He returns for me. And if I am given a chance, I will proclaim His name with my last breath, for He is worthy of all the praise and honor and glory. Thank you Lord, I will never be satisfied until I awake in your likeness. If you are reading this and you have not given your heart to the Lord Jesus Christ, do not tarry for His coming is near and the only other option is Hell!

CONCLUSION

The emptiness that we all feel in our lives is just the absence of our Creator. Living a life without the one who created us is just an empty existence. We spend our lives searching for love in a world that only offers us temporary relief. Those who find happiness outside "The Creator" are just living their days in deception. We are children of light living in darkness until we accept the truth.

America was founded on biblical principles and has reaped the blessings from the God who gives generously to His children. But, each generation seems to be distancing themselves more and more from "One Nation Under God". Those who formed this country were Christians who believed in the Bible and feared God. Today it is hard to identify us as a Christian country. We have taken any sign of Christianity out of our schools. Those who do stand up as born again Christians are persecuted.

Filling the void in our lives is so simple that we don't understand. Jesus came to earth and died on a cross for our sins. He shed His blood for one reason so that we could have a chance to have eternal life. He now resides in Heaven at the right hand of the Father. We don't have to be perfect. In fact, we will never be perfect. All we have to do is believe, receive and turn. God will take our lives and mold us into what He wants us to be.

The problem arises when humans think they must fix themselves or somehow meet a standard. The standard is the world's perception. We have to be willing to accept the gift of salvation. That is all! Then God will step in and finish the job. Most of my life was spent living in a world that offered only glimpses of hope. Once I started looking past my selfishness was when my life really began to improve. Eventually, I came to a crossroads where my quest to fill the void was overshadowed by the light Jesus Christ.

I won't say that every step has been easy; but, I will say that it has been wonderfully fulfilling. I continue to seek a closer relationship with my God. He continues to mold me into the person I so desperately hope to be someday. Thank God for His grace and mercy because without it I would have failed already. My Love deepens for Him with every passing day.

My walk with the Lord continues to astound and excite me. I look forward to attending church with anticipation and expectation. My life is not perfect; but, I strive to please my God every day. The changes I have made are many; but, so rewarding and welcomed. My Sundays are now spent honoring and worshiping the Lord in spirit and in truth. My mind goes back often to the words several days before my precious husband went home to be with the Lord. He said, "God is going to be good to you." He knew, because he had made his peace with the Lord. He had gotten the peace that allowed him to leave this world assured that we would be together again in the kingdom of God.

This journey continues to be one of excitement, challenges and blessings. I am so looking forward to every day because I make Jesus the biggest part of my day. I have had struggles and disappointments over the past few years. They have made me stronger and given me the opportunity to grow in God's love. The most exciting part of this journey is how God is using me to bring others to salvation. Some Christians never get this opportunity or seek it. I continue to seek the Lord with a passion that will never cease until I stand by His side. He said he would never leave me nor forsake me. I say, I will never leave Him nor forsake Him. He says, "Ask and you shall receive". I say, "Lord, ask of me and YOU shall receive. I will be obedient and faithful to my Lord for eternity. I know that in the days and years to come that He will hold me up and comfort me with His mighty hand. I will never stray from His presence; because He says draw near to me and I will draw near to you. I stand on His promises and He is faithful to supply.

I make sure that every day I spend quality time with the Lord. My prayers are frequent and consistent. This is amazing because just a few years ago prayer was an unknown entity. My praise is often and always done in spirit and in truth. My hunger is still for more of the Lord. His Word speaks to me as if He is setting right beside me. This is also amazing given that just a few years ago it was just a book I could not understand.

"My greatest desire is to please the Lord. He said, Go into all the world, and preach the gospel to every creature" (Mark 16: 15). Go therefore, and teach all nations, baptizing, them in the name of the Father, the Son, and the Holy Ghost. Teaching them to observe all things whatsoever I have commanded you, and I am with you always, even unto the end of the world." (Matthew 28:19-20). As Christians this is God's command that we preach the gospel to all who will listen.

I understand why people do not seek much because they do not want to be asked much. "But he that knew not, and did commit things worthy of stripes, shall be beaten with few *stripes*. **For unto whomsoever much is given, of him shall be much required**: and to whom men have committed much, of him they will ask the more" (Luke 12: 48). I truly believe that this life I live is just a vapor and my true life exists beyond that vapor; therefore, I must work until He comes. God's Word states in 1 Thessalonians 4:13, 1 Corinthians 12:1, Romans 1:13 and 11:25 that He does not want us ignorant. To pursue God should be a natural attribute of a Christian. Some Christians seek to hold onto the world and become comfortable that they will go to heaven. "For what shall it profit a man, if he shall gain the whole world and lose his own soul?" (Mark 8:36).

Oh, how I pray that everyone could experience the inspiration and revelation I have received. My God is your God and loves you as He loves me. I just want to shout from the housetops and proclaim to the world that He is the Lord your God. The kingdom of heaven is at hand. He never promised that the cross would not be heavy; but, He said take up your cross and follow me.

I spend each and every day seeking more. My purpose is clear for He is a mighty God who gives revelation to those who are obedient and faithful. The greatest gift is Love and He is the personification of everlasting Love. My journey continues to be full of inspiration and revelation. I know this is a journey on my way to my final destination. A journey may at times get difficult; but, I know that my God has a plan for me and I intend to do my part to fulfill that plan.

I have no doubt that this is not my home. I strive each day to bring my soul and spirit together. My desire is to have less of me and more of the Spirit of God. His Word is alive and speaks to me and feeds my Spirit just as I give food to my body. My desire also is to bring my flesh into submission. This is difficult to do. I am so grateful that I do not have to do it alone.

Because we can never be perfect, I thank God for Grace. The only thing we have for sure is our testimony of how God changed our lives. Hold on to that and cherish it and stand on His promises for He is a faithful God who is the same yesterday, today and for evermore. Place all your hope and trust in the only living God who gave His only Son to die on the cross for our sin. God has given us instructions and a way to be sure of our eternal life. All we have to do is believe, seek and serve. Love the Lord your God with all your heart, with all your mind, with all your soul and with all your strength and love your neighbor as yourself. That's it! Oh, and remember you do not have to do it on your own; you have the Holy Spirit who lives inside you to strengthen you.

Everyone who has a breath has a longing for something to fill the emptiness that dwells in each of us. We try to fill this emptiness with anything that will give us temporary relief. What causes this emptiness? The answer is that we lack a purpose for our life. Once we find that purpose we are made whole. We are children of light living in a world that provides us with temptations that keep us blind and bound in the dark.

I lived in the darkness until my world was shattered by one phone call and one summer that changed my life forever. The quest to fill the void led me from darkness into the marvelous light. Everyone is given the opportunity to experience a greater purpose than just existence.

When you come to the end of your life it is not what you leave behind, but what you take with you that is important. What if you could know for sure what is waiting for you when you step out of this world? You can. But, it involves a quest for the truth. The truth will set you free from bondage and the deception that every human falls victim too. The void in our lives can be filled with the love that we all spend our lives trying to find.